Outsourcing Clinical Development

Outsourcing Clinical Development

Strategies for Working with CROs and Other Partners

Edited by Jane E. Winter and Jane Baguley

Co-published in association with the Pharmaceutical Contract Management Group

Routledge
Taylor & Francis Group
LONDON AND NEW YORK

PCMG
Pharmaceutical Contract Management Group

First published in paperback 2024

First published 2006 by Gower Publishing

Published 2016 by Routledge
4 Park Square, Milton Park, Abingdon, Oxon OX14 4RN

and by Routledge
605 Third Avenue, New York, NY 10158

Routledge is an imprint of the Taylor & Francis Group, an informa business

Publisher's Note
The publisher has gone to great lengths to ensure the quality of this reprint but points out that some imperfections in the original copies may be apparent.

British Library Cataloguing in Publication Data
Outsourcing clinical development: strategies for working
with CROs and other partners
1. Pharmaceutical industry – management 2. Contracting out
I. Winter, Jane II. Baguley, Jane III. Pharmaceutical Contract
Management Group
338.4'76151'0684

Library of Congress Cataloging-in-Publication Data
Outsourcing clinical development : strategies for working with CROs and other partners /
edited by Jane Winter and Jane Baguley.
p. cm.
Includes bibliographical references.
ISBN 0-566-08686-7
1. Drugs--Research. 2. Drug development. 3. Contracting out. 4. Pharmaceutical
industry. I. Winter, Jane, 1960- II. Baguley, Jane.
[DNLM: 1. Drug Industry--organization & administration. 2. Outsourced
Services--organization & administration. 3. Interprofessional Relations. 4. Outsourced
Services--methods. QV 736 O94 2006]
RM301.25.O92 2006
338.4'76151--dc22 2005053087

ISBN 13: 978-0-566-08686-1 (hbk)
ISBN 13: 978-1-03-283775-8 (pbk)
ISBN 13: 978-1-315-59925-0 (ebk)

DOI: 10.4324/9781315599250

Typeset in Bembo by IML Typographers, Birkenhead

Contents

List of Figures

List of Tables

About the Contributors

Jim Cannon specialises in organisation development and has consulted across North America, Europe and Asia. Jim both works as a coach to individual executives and facilitates events designed to improve the effectiveness of teams and organisations. He runs an extensive range of training courses for the Chartered Institute of Personnel and Development and other organisations.

In 1989 Jim started his own consultancy and co-founded Cavendish Partners, now merged with Right Coutts, a firm specialising in career counselling and coaching. He has written several books including *Cost Effective Personnel Decisions* and *Giving Feedback* and workbooks such as *Team-Based Problem Solving*.

Jim has a degree in Behavioural Science, a Masters degree in Manpower studies and a PhD in self-employment.

Michelle Cuddigan is a managing consultant working in the IBM Business Consulting Services Life Sciences team in the UK. Michelle has more than 15 years' experience working in and with the pharmaceutical R&D sector. She has worked with a range of clients in the areas of R&D resourcing, outsourcing strategy, performance management, and organisational change. Michelle has a Pharmacy degree from Trinity College Dublin and also holds an MBA.

Smita Desai is Vice President, Business Development & Business Services Europe, Quintiles Ltd. A qualified pharmacist, Smita has 20 years' experience in the UK and global healthcare industry. Commencing in sales with GlaxoSmithKline (GSK), Smita gained extensive marketing experience in product management roles within GSK and underpinned this with a marketing degree. A ten-year period in international healthcare communications gained through Edelman Worldwide and The Shire Hall Group followed. This enabled invaluable experience to be gained in strategic planning, professional relations, patient advocacy management and public and government affairs management.

Smita joined Quintiles in 1999 responsible for Strategic Business Development. Her current role as head of the European product development business development function has enabled her to build upon her career experience. Her role combines strategic planning and management of Quintiles' European BD function, with strategic involvement with a number of key customers.

John C. Easton is the Director, Global Clinical Outsourcing for AstraZeneca, responsible for leading the R&D outsourcing community in AstraZeneca which in turn manages external delivery of Phase I-IIIB studies through a limited number of preferred providers.

John began his industry career in 1985 as a CRA with May & Baker (Rhone Poulenc). In 1988, he co-founded the CRO Campbell Charles Associates, later working for BIOS before moving to Omnicare Clinical Research in 1996 where he held the positions of Vice President, Business Development Europe, Vice President Worldwide Sales Administration and General Manager for Northern Europe.

Before joining AstraZeneca in 2004, John lived in the US where he was Vice President, Worldwide Account Management at PAREXEL.

John holds a BSc and PhD from the University of London.

Jean S. Edwards is the European Procurement Executive, Eli Lilly & Company Ltd. Jean joined the Procurement Team at Eli Lilly in October 2002 and is responsible for the coordination of clinical outsourcing across Europe and ensuring that Lilly gets best value from their clinical suppliers.

Prior to joining Lilly, Jean spent most of her career with Bayer working in Clinical Research, Quality Management and Contract Resource Management Groups. In her last 18 months at Bayer, Jean was part of the Global External Supplier Management Team responsible for Europe & Overseas.

Carl Emerson is Senior Manager in Clinical Procurement for GlaxoSmithKline Biologicals. Carl started his life as a chemist within GSK, and then moved internally to a number of different roles, before commencing his career in contract management within clinical development. After 15 years, he moved to Celltech where he spent four years. At Celltech Carl pioneered contract management within the company as a new function to drive value in the supply of services. In May 2005 he returned to his origins at GSK and joined the vaccines business in Brussels.

Clinical Procurement is a new discipline in GSKBio and Carl is responsible for driving best procurement practice globally for all spend in the clinical area.

Alan Morgan is the Global General Manager of the Phase II-IV business of MDS Pharma Services, responsible for Clinical Operations, Data Management and Biostatistics, Regulatory Affairs, and all the commercial operations of the business in 20 countries. Prior to joining MDS, Alan spent five years with Covance, initially in finance roles, but latterly as General Manager for their Phase II-III business in Europe, Latin America and Asia.

His initial career was in pharma, including seven years with Glaxo Wellcome and ICI Pharmaceuticals in various business financial roles. Alan is a Graduate of the City University Business School in London, a Fellow of the Chartered Association of Certified Accountants in the UK, and is based in Pennsylvania.

Paul Ranson spent the early part of his career as an in-house lawyer for Smith Kline and Merck Sharpe & Dohme. He is a specialist in the commercial business development and regulatory aspects of the above industries. He has written and lectured extensively in legal issues for the sector including on licensing and outsourcing within the sector. His publications include six report-length papers for the FT, Bridgehead and Legalease. He is on the Legal Issues Committee of the ABHI, coordinator of the Ethical Medicines Industry Group (a grouping representing the interests of small pharmaceutical companies) and was a member of a local Ethics Committee for five years.

Emma Sabin has a degree in Applied Biology and a PhD in virology. She has worked in the pharmaceutical industry for ten years, with roles in Data Management, Project Management and Business Development for both pharma and CRO organisations as well as in Medical Education and PR.

Emma joined the Contracts and Outsourcing group at Pfizer in 2002, and, as Director, Regional Site Lead (Sandwich), now manages the Regional Centre team responsible for the global outsourcing of all services associated with early and full development compounds that are developed by the Sandwich site. Emma also fulfils a leadership role with regard to the Contracts and Outsourcing organisation globally.

Jeff Thomis is President, Clinical Development Services & Phase I/Exploratory Medicine, Europe, Quintiles Ltd. He has been in this role since 1998. The role includes selling and delivery services of project management, clinical monitoring data management, statistics, drug safety, regulatory affairs and phase/exploratory medicine.

Before joining Quintiles in 1997 as European Head of Cardiovascular Strategic Business Unit and General Manager of the Benelux office, he spent 21 years at Bristol Myers Squibb in Europe and the United States, and was involved in the successful development of a number of anti-infective and cardiovascular compounds. Positions held at Bristol Myers Squibb were: Assistant Director Clinical Research, Benelux; Director Clinical Research, Scandinavia; Head of Cardiovascular Research, Europe; Head of Medical Development, Europe, and Director Infectious Diseases.

Dr Thomis is a qualified pharmacist with a PhD in pharmaceutical sciences from University of Leuven, Belgium.

Nadia Turner is a pharmacologist with 19 years' experience in the pharmaceutical industry. She has worked in both pre-clinical and clinical research and as a consultant specialising in outsourcing. Nadia joined Zeneca as Development Strategic Sourcing Manager, and following a spell as a Global Development Project Manager, she took up the position of Associate Director, Global Development Sourcing at AstraZeneca leading a cross-functional team to develop and promote sourcing best-practice decision-making, implementation and evaluation across the global organisation. Nadia moved back into Clinical Development in 2002 as Global Account Manager to lead the relationship management with one of AstraZeneca's preferred suppliers – a role she fulfils today. She has latterly been leading a project to evaluate novel sourcing options for AstraZeneca's oncology clinical development portfolio and is currently involved in developing and implementing a new Operating Model for outsourcing within Clinical Development.

Nermeen Varawalla, Vice President Business Development, leads the international (ex-US) business development team at PRA International, a leading CRO. Prior to this, Nermeen was the founder of PerinClinical, an India-focused CRO. Before that she worked with Accenture's Business Strategy Consulting Practice specialising in drug development.

Nermeen received her medical training at the University of Mumbai, India, before being awarded the Rhodes Research Fellowship to the University of Oxford for her doctoral research. Nermeen then practised as an NHS specialist before obtaining her MBA at INSEAD.

Rikke Winther has headed up Lundbeck's pre-clinical and clinical Contract Management function during the last five years, responsible for the outsourcing process, CRO management, preferred provider agreements and the development of future outsourcing strategies. Prior to this, Rikke worked for eight years within clinical bio-analysis/pharmacokinetics and within CRO Project Management, as Asian Business Development Manager and as a Country Manager.

Rikke is a member of the Pharmaceutical Contract Management Group (PCMG) and Pharmaceutical Outsourcing Management Association (POMA) and regularly presents for both groups.

The PCMG would also like to thank Jacqueline Abbas (Kyowa) and Barry Overton (Cambridge Antibody Technology) for their valuable contributions to Chapters 2 and 6.

Foreword*

John C. Easton, *AstraZeneca*

AN HISTORICAL PERSPECTIVE

The original premise for outsourcing was that it allowed a corporation to trade fixed costs for variable costs, so improving leverage on infrastructure and providing an alternative to building in-house capacity to the levels required to meet peaks in demand. This premise had the added upside of removing investment constraints during periods of high growth by facilitating 'instant' access to capacity and it is as valid today as it was 20 years ago.

As the capabilities of service providers grew, so the segment of process or manufacturing in which they specialised became a core competence. Concurrently, their own financial imperatives, together with competitive market forces, drove them to deliver at increasing rates of efficiency with the result that outsourcing became a more cost-effective method of delivery. Thus a further point of leverage was created for customers.

More recently many of the largest corporations, from auto manufacturers to financial institutions, have struggled to respond to major shifts in the global economy and have faced acute financial pressures as a result. They have had to learn a whole new set of skills in order to drive improved bottom-line performance in the face of acute pricing pressure and stagnating sales growth.

Into this 'challenged' environment came the related solutions of extended outsourcing and managed services. These solutions improve balance-sheet metrics (through the sale of pieces of infrastructure and/or staff to a provider, so generating capital), while dramatically changing the relationship between fixed and variable costs (by renting the capability/resources back from the provider) at the same time as benefiting from improved productivity in the delivery of that capability (as the provider drives

* This Foreword is based on an editorial published in *American Pharmaceutical Outsourcing* in January 2005.

'commercial' grade utilisation out of what had previously been an overhead capability). Corporate information systems (IS) and corporate finance functions have operated against a background of provision through managed services for many years. Today, IS managed services is a multi-billion dollar industry worldwide.

OUTSOURCING AS A STRATEGIC ENABLER

Why was outsourcing able to deliver strategic benefit for these corporations? The simple fact is that outsourcing was embedded in their operating model and their outsourcing strategies were continually aligned with strategic business needs. As their needs moved from basic capacity management to meeting shareholder value challenges, so their outsourcing strategies evolved to include increasingly radical solutions.

A good example of this alignment was described recently in the *Wall Street Journal* (13 June 2004). The 'Big Three' auto manufacturers in the US have been facing intense pricing pressure for some time now and as they searched for a way to respond, there emerged a strategic opportunity to leverage low component manufacturing costs in China. However, labour agreements back in the US made it difficult for the auto companies themselves to leverage the opportunity directly. The answer? Make their suppliers manage outsourcing to China on their behalf! The auto companies set the quality standards and the price, but they leave it up to the component suppliers to work out how and where to outsource off-shore in order to meet the two key business needs of their customers – fit-for-purpose quality at the lowest possible cost.

THE STRATEGY GAP IN BIG PHARMA OUTSOURCING

Over the same timeframe as these developments, big pharma has faced most of the same challenges, albeit lagging perhaps a few years behind the sectors identified earlier. The early 1980s saw regulatory data demands burgeoning while resources were hard to come by and leadership teams were unsure of how to manage in such a high demand growth scenario. So the contract research organisations (CROs) concept took root and began to offer legitimate capacity management solutions. Since then, big pharma has made more or less continuous use of traditional CRO services as a tactic in the short-term management of capacity.

Some have also flirted with the concepts of extended outsourcing – a small number of CROs have made acquisitions of part of a customer's infrastructure (in return for a transient guarantee of an associated revenue stream) in order to achieve post-merger consolidation of redundant assets for the customer. And of course, most recently, Wyeth implemented the first significant managed services type solution in clinical outsourcing when Accenture acquired Wyeth's clinical data management function.

But for the most part, our outsourcing strategies are disconnected from our corporate strategies and our outsourcing behaviours remain wedded to the most basic outsourcing modalities.

HOLDING BACK

What is holding us back and preventing us from tapping this potential source of advantage?

First, we tend to dispute the economic dimension of the benefits case for outsourcing. Intuitively, though, the answer is clear – even if compensation structures are equivalent to big pharma, CRO infrastructure and travel policies are generally inferior. CRO management structures are significantly flatter (leading to lower overheads). Furthermore, CROs are expected to perform at much higher levels of productivity than our own functions in order to meet our expectations and in order to generate profit from a workstream that, for us, is an overhead function. Finally, there is a common perception that CROs make big profits but, in reality, CRO margins are of an order of magnitude less than big pharma's. Outsourcing therefore has to be cost effective – according to a recent study by Datamonitor (*Pharma Times*, May 2004), 74% of German companies and 63% of UK companies in the sectors examined outsource primarily to gain economic benefit.

Secondly, our vision of what outsourcing really offers is constrained. The *Engineering Management* magazine of the Institution of Electrical Engineers (IEE) in England recently carried an article on outsourcing in the engineering space – the outsourcing model in their domain is mature and they describe the various dimensions of outsourcing in the following way:

- Outsourcing entails using external providers to perform recurrent, normally internal, activities or to facilitate profound change.
- Providers assume specific authority and deliver defined services, over specified periods, under agreed pricing regimes.
- The primary driver underlying outsourcing is the incessant need to improve competitiveness and to achieve peak performance by using best-in-breed providers in any activity that is amenable to external fulfilment, and is non-core and not a specialism of the customer.

If we run a quick gap analysis between our world and these proven benefits, then the first part of the first statement would certainly be found to be true – we do outsource normally internal, recurrent activities. However, we do not outsource in order to 'facilitate profound change'. From the second statement, we can certainly meet the requirement that our providers deliver defined services, over specified periods, under agreed pricing regimes, but we are not good at delegating specific authority (see later). But the most revealing gap is demonstrated by the final statement which shows a fundamental contradiction in our outsourcing model. We all go to great lengths to select 'best-in-breed providers', and invest in protracted and costly assessments to achieve this, and yet we eventually use them as little more than paid hands.

Finally, the third, and perhaps most critical, driver for the lack of evolution in clinical outsourcing is our internal conflict around core competencies. Datamonitor's report found that 'new breed pharmaceutical companies will succeed only by keeping in-house the intellectual capital critical to success and outsourcing the rest'. Thus the critical question is – which competencies are actually core and critical to success?

Most big pharma have vision and mission statements that are built around 'innovation in product development', 'meeting un-met clinical need', and so on. None of them mention an aspiration to be best in class in running clinical studies – however, this *is* one of the core missions for most clinical CROs. If we look again at the first statement in the UK IEE's definition of outsourcing we see that 'normally internal' functions are outsourced. Inherent in this statement is the assumption that internal capacity in a particular function reduces as outsourcing of that function increases. This has not happened in the case of clinical outsourcing. As a result there is conflict between the competencies that the business model *requires* to be core and those that the grass roots of the organisation *believes* are core.

RECOGNISING OUR NEED

If we look at our own challenges today, they line up with those other industries have faced and dealt with in the last ten years using outsourcing as a part of their response. In 1998, PriceWaterhouseCoopers (now IBM Consulting) identified that the big pharma business model had a longevity issue (in their *Pharma 2005* suite of reports). Their 'Value Builder' model even forecast and modelled the difficulties that we would face in delivering future value to our shareholders. Since then, big pharma sales growth has, in general, slowed while growth rates in R&D expense have been maintained or even accelerated. Share prices for the largest pharma have, in general, fallen and market capitalisation for many big pharma today is lower than it was in 1998. And now, of course, we have the threat of price benchmarking against generic alternatives to add to our challenges.

The responses that we must make have been clear for some considerable time – we must reduce development costs by 30–40 per cent while at the same time significantly shorten development cycle time in order to drive new levels of productivity. These should be the strategic goals to which our outsourcing strategies are aligned.

RESPONDING TO THE CHALLENGE

Pharmaceutical, biotechnology and device company spend on CRO and laboratory services has shown sequential double-digit growth rates for many years now. The market broke through the $10 billion threshold for the first time in 2003 and most analysts forecast continued double-digit growth over the next three to five years. Others forecast significant growth rates in the level of clinical development activity that is outsourced (without attaching dollar estimates), with one observer predicting that the number of companies outsourcing 60–100 per cent of activity will double between 2003 and 2008.

However, if we are successfully to use outsourcing as a vehicle to meet our corporate challenges then the future growth in spend forecast by analysts is going to have to be based on a very different set of drivers than those which created historical growth. Our outsourcing strategies must balance the continually increasing regulatory data burden on drug development with the need to reduce the total costs of development by more than 30 per cent. This offset will not be achieved by simply driving down provider rates – even if we completely removed our provider's profits, we would barely dent the challenge – but instead will require radical delivery solutions. We will need to begin to work with our providers and understand how we can capitalise on their more agile operating models in order to move our own thinking forward. We will (finally) need to address the conflict of competencies discussed earlier and move to a model like that described by the IEE where we use best-in-breed providers to improve competitiveness and performance.

We will, of course, need to ensure that our provider base meets the demands of this new environment. We will also need to build contracting and relationship management tools and processes that can deliver levels of performance and value far beyond those achieved today, and Chapters 2 through to 9 of this book will give you some insight into the latest thinking in these dimensions. However, ultimate success will be driven by outstanding strategy and decision-making – Chapter 1 will help you begin your journey.

CHAPTER 1

Outsourcing Strategies

Jeff Thomis and Smita Desai, *Quintiles Ltd*

Outsourcing is the contracting of any activity or service to a third party (McHugh, Merlin and Wheeler, 1995; Drtina, 1994). The effect of outsourcing on companies is often described as a form of 'vertical disintegration' (Eroglin, 1994; Walker and Weber, 1984).

Outsourcing of goods and services is not new. In the eighteenth and nineteenth centuries, contracting was commonplace in England and included a range of public and private services. However, during the twentieth century internalisation of activities within companies became the dominant trend. Two key factors contributed to this re-internalisation, namely direct government involvement in economic activity and development of production technologies that favoured large, vertically integrated organisations. However, the same factors that forced the initial retreat from outsourcing, ultimately led to its resurgence in the 1980s and 1990s.

It is now argued that in order to achieve a long-term competitive advantage, an enterprise should focus on its core competencies and outsource activities for which it has neither a critical strategic need nor the capabilities (Quinn 1992). However, the problems associated with identifying core competencies, and the dawning that proprietary technical knowledge may not be the central basis for obtaining market leadership, has led to a rethinking of the reasons for outsourcing (Domberger, 1998). Domberger (1998) has argued that a better basis on which to make an outsourcing decision is that of specialisation and hence relative efficiency, leading to improvement in overall competitiveness.

This chapter focuses on pharmaceutical R&D outsourcing and discusses clinical development outsourcing strategies, the challenges of assessing pharma core competencies, strategies for working with contract research organisations (CROs), and last but not least, preferred supplier relationships and strategic outsourcing, the hallmark of future drug development successes. Subjects such as resource planning, insourcing versus outsourcing, decision hierarchy and accountability, importance of geography and potential for offshore sourcing and niche providers are all discussed within this context. Current practices are highlighted and models and best practices suggested whereby improvements upon these practices may be made.

OUTSOURCING OF PHARMACEUTICAL R&D FOCUSING ON CLINICAL DEVELOPMENT

Outsourcing in the pharmaceutical industry has traditionally implied converting the fixed costs of resources and infrastructure assigned to execute development activities, into variable costs. It involved paying a sub-contractor to perform these activities, mostly on an *ad hoc* basis. Such sub-contractors were either contract research organisations (CROs) or contract manufacturing organisations (CMOs). During the process, pharmaceutical companies, however, have always strived to retain the intellectual property associated with in-house product development.

History of clinical development outsourcing

Outsourcing of pharmaceutical R&D began in the 1970s. Although rather little is known about the early history of clinical development outsourcing, it is conceivable that the first areas to be outsourced were back-door and very process-driven activities. One such activity is data management, and in the late 1970s, as demands from regulators increased, so did the need for robust data management processes and the capability for handling larger volumes of data. Not surprisingly then, that this period saw the execution of the first large cardiovascular outcome studies which required the collection of comparable large datasets.

The pharmaceutical industry responded to this increased resourcing need, and projects with lower priority became candidates for outsourcing. At the same time, the need for more proper statistical analyses created a market for statistical consulting which rapidly developed into a new outsourcing market. Dennis Gillings, a professor of statistics at the University of North Carolina, Chapel Hill, and founder, Chairman and CEO of Quintiles, undertook his first consultancy in statistics for a pharmaceutical customer in 1974 and went on to establish Quintiles, an organisation which initially specialised in data management and statistical services, in 1982. Such an initial scenario was confirmed in a *CenterWatch* survey of 15 pharmaceutical companies (1998) in which data collection/monitoring and statistical analysis were identified as the most commonly used services (77 per cent and 57 per cent, respectively) with respect to outsourced projects.

During the 1980s, in the US in particular, the regulatory environment began to change. The Food and Drug Administration (FDA) incorporated the principles of the Belmont Report into the Code of Federal Regulations, passed the Safe Medical Devices Act, the Orphan Drug Act, and became an agency of the Department of Health and Human Services. Pharmaceutical companies began to feel the burden of having to provide increasing amounts of data of regulatory quality in support of each new drug application, and this effectively triggered an increased demand for the outsourcing of some or all of these activities.

Outsourcing of clinical monitoring and site management had an even slower start. The late Hein Besselaar, founder of Besselaar, now part of Covance, and Joe von Rickenbach, CEO of Parexel, were some of the early pioneers in this area, but it is safe to say that initially CROs were seen as 'body shops' or 'capacity for hire' by the pharmaceutical industry. Indeed, it is only really in the last ten years with the maturation of the outsourcing process, that CRO staff are now beginning to be seen as specialists and adding value to the clinical development chain value.

Growing acceptance of outsourcing

After a timid beginning, outsourcing is now well accepted and practised across the pharmaceutical industry. In a recent survey conducted among European-based pharmaceutical companies on behalf of Quintiles (*Datamonitor* 2003), access to superior skills/expertise, cost savings and increase in operational flexibility were identified as the top three outsourcing benefits, benefits shared with IT, financial and telecom industries (Figure 1.1). Similar levels of benefit are seen not only for the outsourcing of clinical development but also in the areas of product commercialisation and promotion.

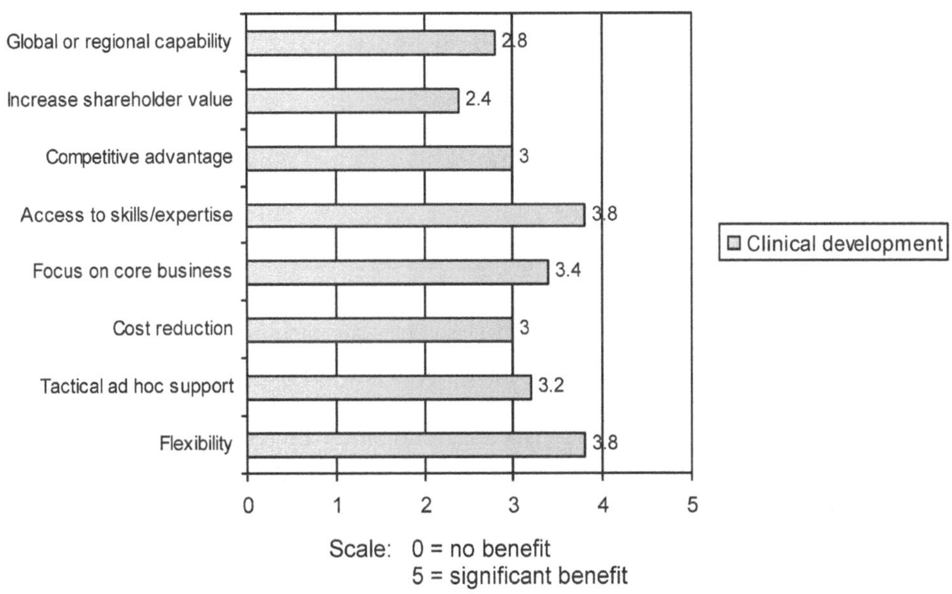

Figure 1.1 Degree of benefit derived from outsourcing clinical development for specific business strategies

Most surveys conducted to-date continue to show that in the main, R&D and clinical development capacity shortfalls remain the principal motivation for outsourcing. Outsourcing is still largely conducted as a means by which the number of desired projects may continue to be carried out, without additional investment in in-house R&D, clinical development staff or infrastructure. Interestingly, 100 per cent of pharmaceutical industry respondents considered outsourcing important and 71 per cent stated that outsourcing will gain in importance in the next three years, a clear confirmation that the outsourcing process is maturing. However, cost, a fear of lack of quality and performance issues are still the main concerns with outsourcing.

Size of the outsourcing market

Although there is agreement that the CRO industry has seen unprecedented growth, reliable numbers are hard to obtain. Numbers of total R&D expenditure vary greatly between different reports, perhaps because some do not include biotech R&D expenditure (Table 1.1). In addition, outsourced penetration and how this divides between the various services (pre-clinical, phase I, II–III, IIIb–IV, central labs) is subject to a lot of interpretation.

Table 1.1 The global pharmaceutical R&D outsourcing market

	1999	2000	2001	2002	2003	2004E	2005E	2006E	2007E
Global R&D ($ bn)	43.7	48.1	56.0	61.1	67.5	76.2	85.5	96.8	109.2
Global development ($ bn)*	31.3	34.8	39.2	42.7	47.3	53.4	59.9	67.7	76.4
Global clinical development ($ bn)**	16.3	18.1	20.4	22.3	24.9	27.4	31.2	35.7	40.6
% Clinical development outsourced	19.8	17.7	21.0	21.5	22.1	22.6	22.1	22.1	22.4
Clinical development 9.1 outsourcing market ($ bn)		3.2	3.2	4.3	4.8	5.5	6.2	6.9	7.9

*Fixed rate of 70%

** Clinical development defined as phases I–IV inclusive plus laboratory services

Source: Goldman Sachs, PhRMA, EFPIA and author's estimates and analyses

One source estimates the global pharmaceutical and biotech R&D spend to be $76 bn in 2004, the development spend to be $53 bn and the outsourced market to be $11.4 bn (Goldman Sachs, 2004).

As would be expected given the fragmented nature of the CRO market and multiple definitions of outsourcing, analyst estimates of the size of the R&D and clinical outsourced development market vary. However, it is a recognisable trend that pharma companies are generally outsourcing a greater proportion of their clinical development work (Table 1.2).

Estimates of the overall penetration of outsourcing in clinical development was 21 per cent in 2004, with penetration of 95 per cent in central labs, 25 per cent in phase IIIb–IV, 16 per cent in phase I and 15 per cent in phase II–III.

Table 1.2 Global clinical development outsourcing market ($ bn) by phase, 2001–2007

	2001	2002	2003	2004E	2005E	2006E	2007E
Global clinical development	4.3	4.8	5.5	6.2	6.9	7.9	9.1
Phase I	0.5	0.5	0.6	0.7	0.8	0.9	1.0
Phase II–III	1.7	1.9	2.1	2.2	2.3	2.6	2.9
Phase IIIb–IV	1.1	1.3	1.6	1.9	2.3	2.7	3.2
Central laboratories	1.0	1.1	1.2	1.4	1.5	1.7	2.0

Outsourcing penetration is forecast to increase further, to an estimated 22.8 per cent in 2007 (Goldman Sachs, 2000, 2003), underscored by a favourable mix shift towards biotech, and growing economic justification for pharma to increase the percentage of their outsourced drug development.

The CRO industry has grown to meet the increasing demand, and it is currently estimated that the number of CROs worldwide has now reached over 1000 in spite of continued consolidation in recent years.

CROs now offer a wide range of services, from early development through clinical development and to late phase services. Some, such as Quintiles, are also able to provide services extending beyond drug development into drug commercialisation, as outlined in Figure 1.2.

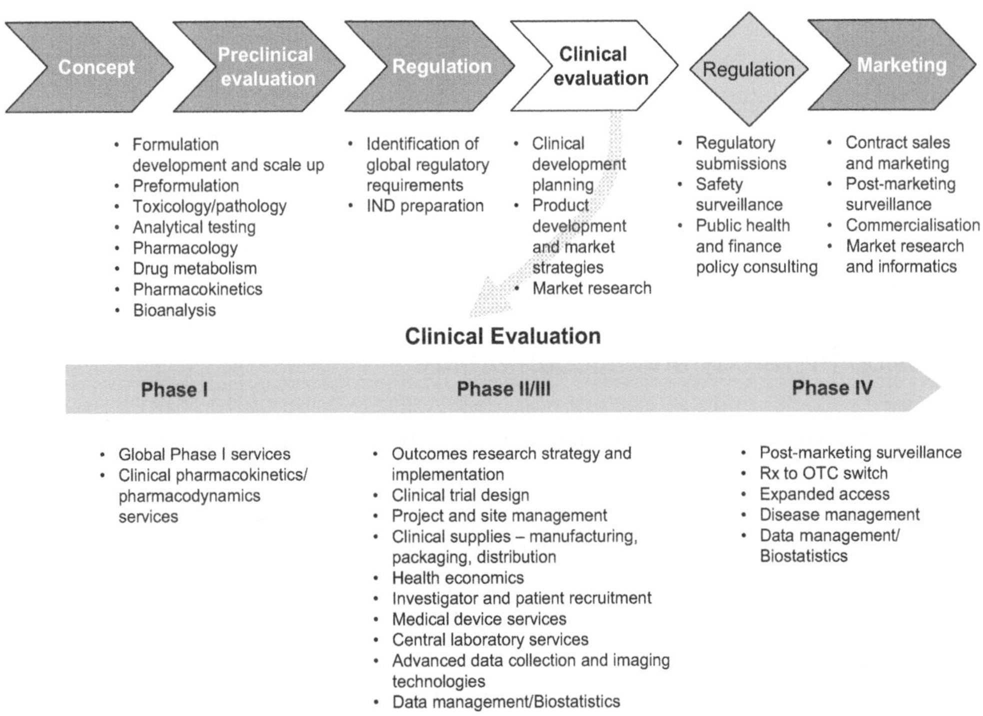

Figure 1.2 Typical full service CRO services

In addition, the larger CROs are able to leverage their geographic coverage and their intellectual property to the strategic advantage of the pharmaceutical sector. Fluctuating drug development pipelines and high levels of product attrition still bedevil many pharma companies and with drug development costs still rising inexorably, many continue to search for more cost-effective and speedier solutions.

CROs which have a large global footprint are able to source and deliver large patient pools quickly, accessing these from research-naïve, yet populous, regions such as Central and Eastern Europe, Asia Pacific, India, China and Africa. They have been instrumental in driving training, accreditation, and increasing acceptance by regulatory authorities such as EMEA and FDA of data generated in these regions. In effect, they have paved the way for the inclusion of these regions into global medical R&D. Furthermore, many of the global CROs are leveraging the lower cost of the highly educated labour infrastructure in these regions to provide 'back room' services such as data entry and IT.

CROs are increasingly able to provide the pharma sector with significant strategic benefit, flexing their global footprints to achieve speedier, more cost-effective drug development. Some CROs are even taking this one step further facilitating risk mitigation during the drug development process, a topic we will return to later in this chapter.

OUTSOURCING STRATEGIES

Most pharmaceutical companies, irrespective of size, do not have a robust, strategically focused, outsourcing strategy. Portfolio management and headcount freezes continue to provide the rationale for outsourcing, sourced and fulfilled, mostly in an *ad hoc* manner.

Outsourcing continues to be viewed as an execution solution when the internal organisation cannot resource the study or project or when affiliates consider it of less importance for local business purposes.

Outsourcing strategies can take different forms and shapes. The starting point, however, is the fundamental decision about whether to insource or outsource.

Decision hierarchy and accountability

The typical pharma clinical development decision tree for sourcing additional capacity is depicted in Figure 1.3.

The decision to either undertake a given clinical development activity internally or externally is, in most companies, a complex interaction between central R&D, local R&D or medical affairs, the central marketing department, affiliate companies and finance groups. Very often budgets for outsourced work, whether as a percentage of development spend or a dollar value, are agreed annually, and are driven by the need for short-term resources. Such a decision tree, and the budgetary process underpinning this sort of decision-making, is typical for tactical outsourcing.

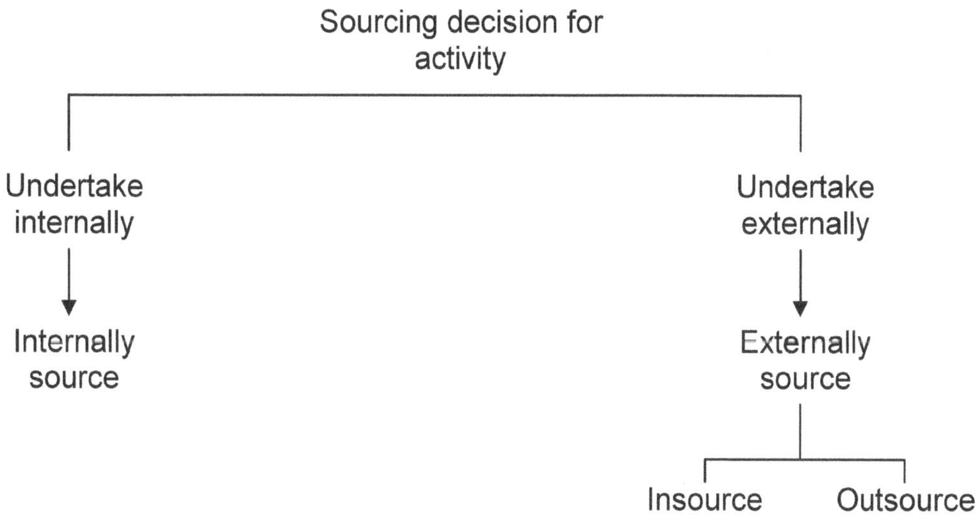

Figure 1.3 Sourcing decision tree

The underlying characteristics of tactical outsourcing are that of a typical buyer-seller relationship for any kind of service or product. They are mostly controlled by a detailed scope of work and rigid contracts. They are mostly short-term in nature, although preferred provider agreements (PPAs) do often contain a promise for repeated work against the extraction of a volume discount or fixed and/or reduced hourly charge-out rates per resource category and definitions of hours spent on individual tasks. Value, in terms of how the CRO can deliver genuine added value rather than just vaguely defined values, such as therapeutic area expertise, tends not to be a consideration.

Accountability for tactical outsourcing, including PPAs, often lies with the outsourcing department, with or without tactical direction from corporate procurement and clinical development operational teams. Most companies have therefore set up cross-functional teams with clear roles and responsibilities, and with processes and practices for the selection of key suppliers in place. The relative roles of the outsourcing department, operational teams and corporate procurement will vary greatly across organisations and will largely depend on their responsibilities. When their responsibilities are clearly defined a Responsible Accountable Supports Consulted Informed (or RASCI) chart can be a useful tool, completed and shared across the clinical development organisation and other departments involved in the outsourcing process. An example of a RASCI chart is provided in Table 1.3.

Inevitably, in a highly tactical outsourcing environment, where emphasis on cost reduction is paramount, the prominence, influence and enhanced role of procurement departments often takes a dominant position.

Insourcing, outsourcing and hybrids

Traditionally a difference is made between insourcing, that is, staff brought in from an external organisation to satisfy capacity needs, and outsourcing, that is, work placed wholly with an external organisation to satisfy capacity needs. From these definitions one

Table 1.3 Example of RASCI Chart

	Sourcing/outsourcing department	Operational teams department	Procurement
Sourcing decision	RA	SCI	
Select CRO	RA	SCI	I
Price/contracts negotiation	RA	I	SC
Manage project deliverables	SC	RA	I
Manage relationship	RA	SCI	

Key: R(esponsible) A(ccountable) S(upports) C(onsulted) I(nformed)

would assume there is no difference between both forms of resourcing, as both require interaction with an external organisation. There is, however, a fundamental difference in so far as insourced staff are contracted and in essence the contractual agreement is very similar to that of a temporary worker. It makes sense, therefore, that insourcing is often referred to as customer managed. Outsourced work in contrast is characterised by a contractual agreement derived around a scope of service provision over a defined period of time, and delivered according to a number of key milestones and quality standards.

The growth of companies providing insourced services is a sign that customers have adopted this strategy. Such companies range from CROs, to temporary staffing agencies and independent contractors. The benefits of using temporary employees include cost and the ability to staff up quickly. The trade-off is the effort spent on training. In addition, if you bring in too many temporary personnel, they effectively become a fixed rather than a variable resource.

One of the issues with this type of arrangement is the labour legislation in place in a number of European countries (Table 1.4). Several EU countries have legislation in place

Table 1.4 EU countries' legal framework on temporary workers

Countries with specific legislation on temporary workers	Countries with specific intersectorial and sectoral collective agreements applicable for temporary workers	Countries with few or no specific legislation on temporary workers
Austria	Belgium	Denmark
Belgium	Finland	Finland
France	France	Greece
Germany	Germany	Ireland
Italy	Italy	Sweden
Netherland	Netherland	United Kingdom
Norway	Spain	
Portugal	Norway (foreseeable)	
Spain		

which, unless the provider is registered as a temporary work agency, temporary workers, for example, customer managed staff, could claim equal status to that of pharma staff with its effect on salary and benefit packages.

Several attempts have been made to agree on an EU Directive for temporary workers, but all have failed including the last in 2004 during the Dutch presidency. It is believed that several countries will now put in place local legislation similar to the failed EU Directive on temporary workers.

Not surprisingly, given the complex employer legislation considerations associated with insourcing options, a series of hybrid solutions has also evolved between insourcing and outsourcing. One such example sees insourced staff based in another office and line managed by the internal organisation, but working exclusively on one project or for one customer. This and other forms of insourcing are very popular with certain pharmaceutical companies and in certain countries. It gives pharma the flexibility to bring in staff whenever needed, keep direct control on their activities and all this usually at a reduced cost. It provides them with a pool of staff from which they can recruit if their headcount requirement alters. In addition, by employing only insourced staff they are moving fixed costs to variable costs, something which will show in their balance sheets and metrics. Apart from the liability danger, it is a modified form of internalisation and does not fit with optimal capability sourcing.

Outsourcing can take place within a number of different operating and contractual frameworks, as depicted in Figure 1.4.

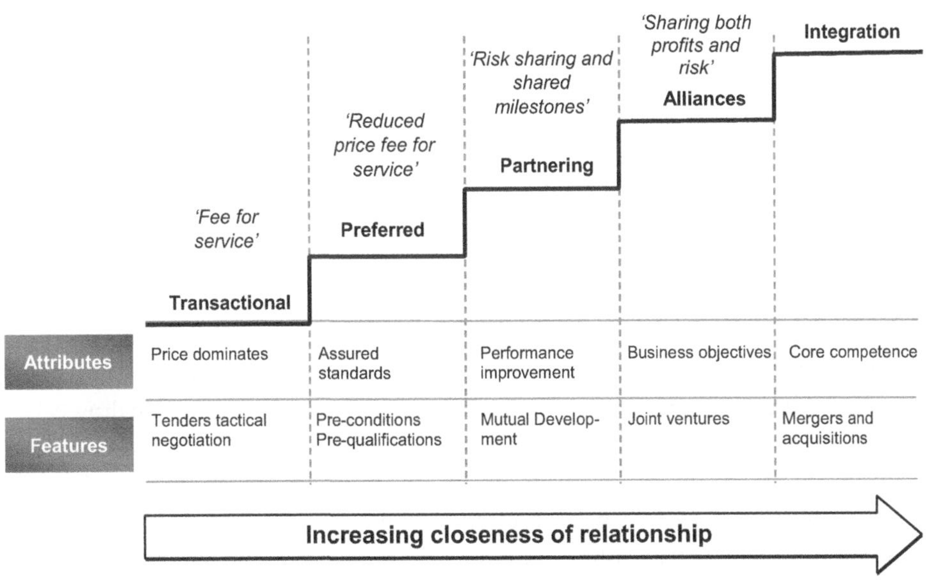

Figure 1.4 Possible operating and contractual outsourcing frameworks
Source: PriceWaterhouseCoopers

These are often viewed as a step-wise progression from a transactional relationship between a pharma client and a CRO to, ultimately, one of a strategic alliance underscored by risk mitigation by both parties. There are different levels of supplier relationship, any of which are valid under the right circumstances. Such a progression demands a considerable level of trust, candour and transparency between the two organisations. Operating practices, cultures and behaviours will need to change, often causing short-term corporate angst within a pharma company.

The rewards, however, are considerable, and at their most simple, promise the expansion of the development budget, and therein corporate ability to pursue a greater number of development opportunities in a cost-efficient and cost-effective manner. Development risk may be mitigated and often development timelines accelerated providing further promise of enhanced competitive advantage. Table 1.5 outlines the potential benefits of the various operating and contractual outsourcing models.

Table 1.5 Benefits of outsourcing models

Model	Potential benefits
Transactional outsourcing	• Capacity management
Preferred partnerships	• Reduced costs associated with CRO management • Enhanced operational efficiencies in line with volume resources
Strategic partnerships	• Shared goals and objectives • Optimal proactive resource management • Knowledge transfer • Shared technologies and processes leading to further enhanced operational efficiencies
Strategic alliances	• Stringent removal of redundant or duplicate cost • Enhanced productivity • Risk share for development projects • Mutual and converging organisational development

Currently the majority of pharma outsourcing lies within the transactional arena. That said, the last two years have seen an acceleration towards securing preferred partnership arrangements, spurred on no doubt by the need to 'fix drug development' costs as far as possible for the foreseeable future.

While this progression is to be applauded it remains to be seen whether such moves will be sufficient for the industry to really address their key issue – unsustainable drug development budgets.

Precedence has shown that the benefits of outsourcing increase exponentially as one progresses through the relationship continuum. It is the desire, and indeed the frustration of the CRO industry, that to date only a handful of pharma companies have embraced strategic outsourcing in full and to its greatest benefit.

It is to be hoped that the current trend towards PPAs will serve to furnish confidence within the pharma sector of the benefits of strategically aligned relationships and therein underscore a desire to accelerate the benefits that can be accrued when this develops into a full strategic partnership or strategic alliance.

STRATEGIES FOR WORKING WITH CROS

The success or failure of an outsourcing activity is not solely dependent on the criteria used to make the outsourcing decision. Processes and systems are needed to manage the relationship and control the outsourced activities. Contracts, communication channels and performance monitoring seem to be the most important management mechanisms for both tactical outsourcing and PPA environments.

The contract

The contract provides the opportunity for pharma and CRO to agree on how a range of issues will be managed before the work passes to the outsourcer. Typically, a contract will specify the obligations that each party has to the other. The most important contractual elements can be broadly divided up into terms and conditions, scope of work and financials. Figure 1.5 depicts the most important contractual elements.

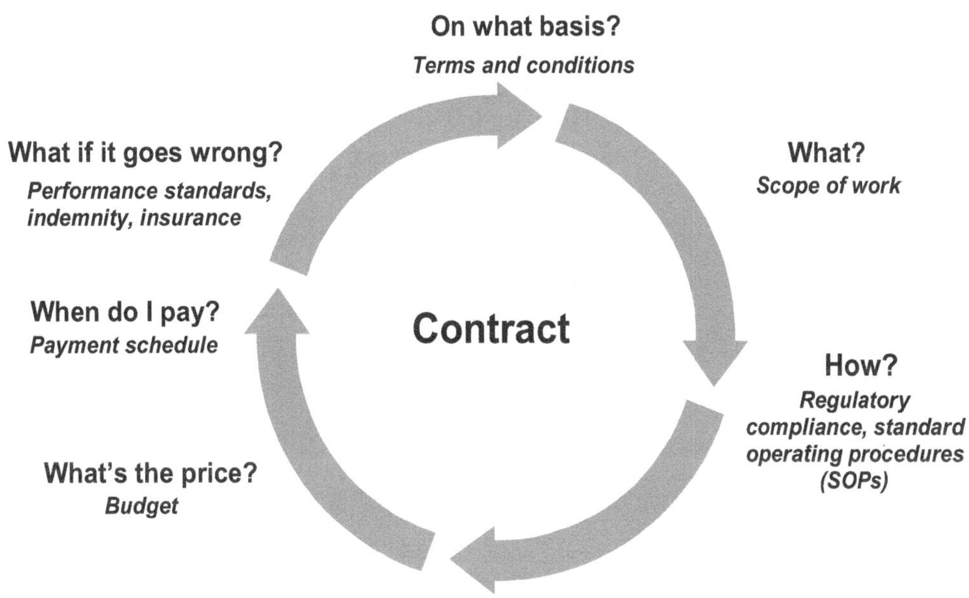

Figure 1.5 Contractual elements

However, it is difficult to include all of the important aspects within a contract without it becoming too cumbersome and inflexible. In addition, it is difficult to foresee all contingencies that may arise during the course of the project and include them within the formal agreement. Therefore, the contract is only the starting point in setting up systems to manage the outsourcing relationship.

Communication channels

An important aspect of effective relationship management is the establishment of a 'protocol' for communication between the parties. While ideally relationships need to develop between pharma and CROs at many levels, to avoid a myriad of communication channels leading to confusion, there needs initially to be a single point of contact and usually that will be the two project managers or staff with a similar assignment. In addition, there is a relationship between the outsourcing department and the contracts and/or business development department or staff with that responsibility. A process of conflict resolution should also be agreed, involving senior management from both pharma and CRO.

Usually PPAs foresee the establishment of a relationship management model consisting of a series of committees with memberships from pharma and the CRO. These usually include a governance or steering committee and an operations committee. An example is depicted in Figure 1.6. The governance/steering committee is usually responsible for strategic direction and executive oversight of the pharma–CRO relationship. Apart from setting strategic direction, it ensures optimal resource planning and high-level issue resolution. It usually meets quarterly initially and thereafter, as required. The operational committee forms the core of the PPA relationship management. It ensures setting of operational standards and appropriate resource management across projects, and issue resolution. Initially it meets monthly and thereafter quarterly. The project teams are responsible for project planning and execution, and these meet on an ongoing basis.

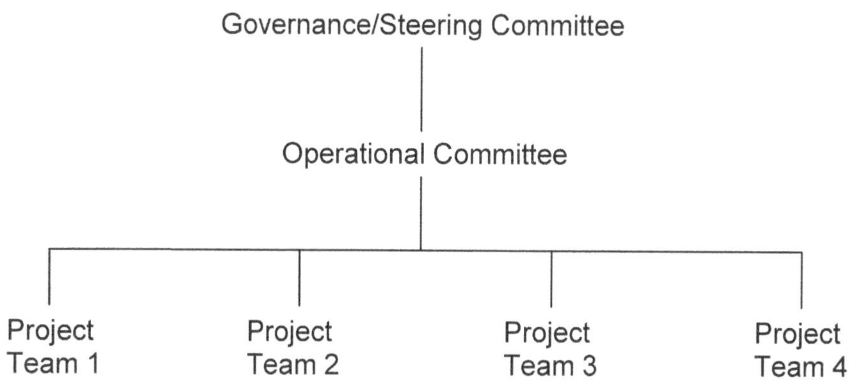

Figure 1.6 Preferred provider agreement relationship management model

Performance monitoring

Monitoring of performance of tasks, project or function being outsourced as well as of the relationship throughout the contract is desirable and can be achieved through the use of performance metrics and benchmarks which focus on areas of delivery responsiveness, service quality, cost and customer satisfaction. This could include a balanced scorecard to monitor delivery (Figure 1.7).

These scorecards should be simple so that the effort required for data collection is not too cumbersome and to ensure their continued use. These metrics are primarily aimed at measuring CRO performance, but it would also be useful to measure pharma performance. This requires a significant level of trust as CRO staff may be reluctant to provide honest feedback if this would jeopardise the prospect of repeat business. The performance metrics and time of measurements should be defined in the contract or agreed shortly after initiation of the project so that expectations are clear and understood.

Index	Goal # 1	Goal # 2
Financial	Reduction of cycle time by 15%	Minimise cost per subject from study 1 to 2 by 15%
Internal	Defect target of less than 10%	Costs associated with re-work not to exceed 0.1% of total budget
Customer	CFS score of 8 or more	Loyalty and trust index
People	Fill vacancies within 30 days of award	Employee retention rate of 90%

Figure 1.7 Balanced scorecard

Internal costs of outsourcing

One area that is usually overlooked is the internal cost of managing outsourcing, particularly the internal costs associated with CRO selection, relationship management and project management. These incremental costs have been estimated to be 12–16 per cent of the CRO contracted value, but in reality will be closer to 25–30 per cent. It is not an exception for pharma to use more than 100 service providers for their R&D activities and it is clear that the incremental cost is directly related to the number of providers.

Furthermore, another, often hidden, internal cost is that incurred due to the need to establish contact with investigators and key opinion leaders (KOLs) other than as part of the clinical development process. During clinical development, there is usually regular contact between pharma staff, KOLs and investigators. Pharma staff will regularly consult KOLs for advice on trial results and to give presentations at conferences deemed important for medical marketing purposes. These activities should continue during outsourcing, but will in most cases require pharma resources.

Leveraging geography and low-cost off-shoring

Traditionally, clinical development activities have been undertaken in North America, Western Europe and Japan. The main reason(s) for this are that when combined, these regions represent 80 per cent of the pharmaceutical market. In addition, they have had an abundance of qualified investigators, qualified pharma and CRO staff, as well as sufficient numbers of suitable patients. However, a number of factors have forced both pharma and the CRO industry to look at other suitable geographic regions:

- The growing need for large numbers of clinical trial patients.
- The considerable cost of conducting clinical development programmes in North America, Western Europe and Japan.

- The ethical climate which makes the conduct of placebo controlled and treatment naïve studies much more difficult.

The first geographic region that became of interest was Eastern Europe. The fall of the Berlin wall and the demise of the communist regimes in a number of countries opened this area for clinical development. The proximity to Western Europe, the high standard of medical care before the Second World War, the eagerness of the medical community and interest of patients to have access to new drugs made this area very interesting. A few pharma companies established clinical research facilities in various countries starting with Poland, Hungary and the Czech Republic and moving slowly further to the East. The large CROs quickly followed suit and Quintiles established their first presence in 1995.

The move for drug development to be conducted in Eastern Europe was quickly followed with an acknowledgement of the relative attractiveness of Latin America, India and lately China as drug development regions of increasing importance (Figure 1.8). Much of the attractiveness for different regions is associated with the view that the primary reason for doing studies in these geographic areas is the potential for cost savings. Others, however, believe that these savings are only achievable once you are set up there in the region.

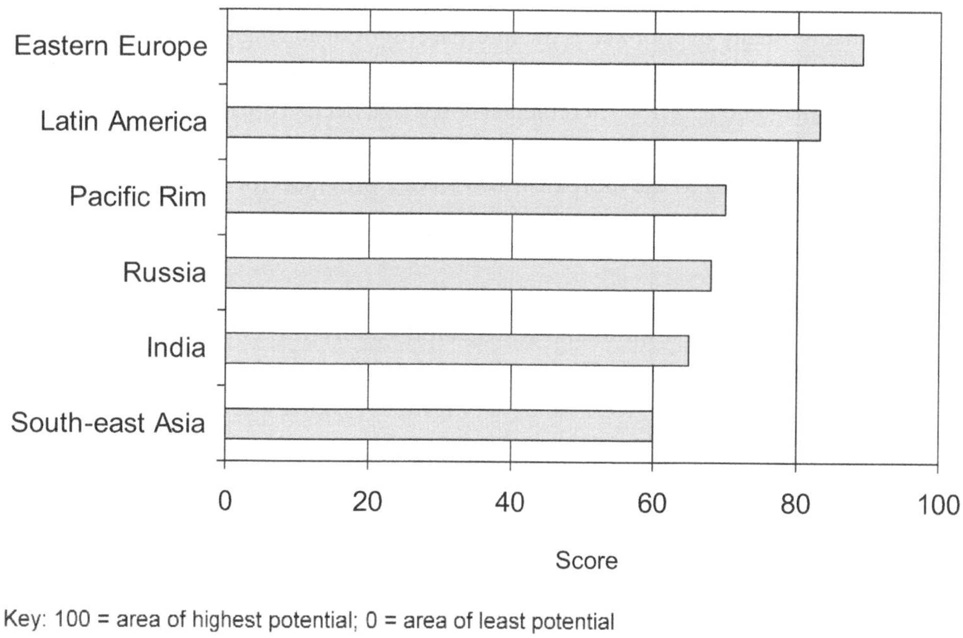

Figure 1.8 Attractiveness of geographic regions for patient recruitment
Source: Tufts Center for the Study of Drug Development (2004)

It is also important to remember that the regulatory environment of these regions is not static. In India, for example, a government decree issued in December 2004 has brought the country's patent laws into compliance with the World Trade Organisation and will undoubtedly spur clinical research. However, at the same time, the Indian authorities have proposed changes in the regulations governing drug testing, emphasising compliance with International Conference on Harmonisation Guidelines on Good Clinical Practice (ICH-GCP) guidelines. These changes will make placebo-controlled studies more difficult to conduct and delay regulatory approvals. In addition, the dietary differences with the West, and the yet unknown genetic and proteomic diversity of these populations compared to the West, will cause pharma companies to carefully consider how much of their pivotal work can be placed in these countries. Generally, pharma executives have stated that they are prepared to recruit up to 30 per cent of its trial patients from these areas for their clinical development programmes.

Niche providers

Niche clinical development providers are CROs that provide either a limited number of clinical development services in a limited geographic area or a broad range of activities in a very restricted geography. A 2001 *CenterWatch* survey on quality found that small- and medium-sized CROs were more responsive, more accessible and less bureaucratic than larger CROs. It has therefore been argued that the model of CROs that encompasses a broad range of services and a global footprint can readily be challenged by networks of niche and small-sized CROs with high quality of service and constant innovative operations working within a smaller infrastructure base (Bowden and MacKenzie-Lawrie, 2002; King and Cuddigan, 2003; Lacey, 2003; Law, 2004). Reference is made to other industries, where such a network of suppliers is very common if not the rule. In these industries, organisations surround themselves with a network of specialised best-in-class providers. Cost savings are significant and similar degrees of increases in quality and throughput are observed. These networks are led by effective and innovative project management and use effective communications technologies. It is also argued that small CROs have the ability to attract and recruit good staff from large CROs, and leverage technology faster. They are therefore well placed to create a varied, multi-tasking environment in which to gain expertise and accumulate experience. Such a prospect is a considerable attraction to many CRO staff in this increasingly knowledge-based industry.

In 2004, a number of small service and niche providers formed a trade group, Clinical Providers Consortium (CPC), to compete with the large CRO's trade group, the Association of Clinical Research Organisations (ACRO). This step is indicative of the determination of the niche providers to look after their own interests and to be able to compete with large CRO's broad service offerings.

These factors notwithstanding, it is interesting to note, however, that three years on from this prediction, the market share of the large CROs has, if anything, increased further. A number of large CROs have set up agreements with niche CROs in geographic areas where they previously had no presence, particularly outside North America and Western Europe. In addition, large CROs have shifted their value proposition away from only providing resources towards sourcing patients and delivering studies efficiently and effectively. Global presence has been a key enabler in this shift and has enabled large CROs to position themselves as solution providers and not just resource providers.

Virtual pharma companies

Virtual pharma companies are a relatively new concept. They are organisations that have a small core of mainly project management specialists and outsource the majority of their capabilities. They are therefore able to promise lower development costs, mainly because of their reduced infrastructure overheads. Experience with such companies is limited, although there are a few examples which seem to suggest that they have a role to play within outsourcing options. A high-profile example is Protodigm Ltd (Fulcrum) which was set up as a subsidiary of Roche UK in 1996. The company tendered for development projects for compounds from Roche in competition with in-house alternatives. They were given three drugs to develop:

- tempium, a phase III drug for Alzheimer's;
- DMDC, a phase II cytidine derivative from Yamasa for cancer; and
- anti-CD18, a phase II recombinant humanised monoclonal antibody for myocardial infarction.

Fulcrum claims that development costs and time were reduced by at least 25 per cent and has produced real-life data of these cost savings for three therapeutic areas (Figure 1.9). However, critics have argued that a small, flexible organisation focused on delivery cost and time efficiencies for a limited number of development programmes would have an easier task to deliver these cost efficiencies than a large multi-national pharmaceutical company.

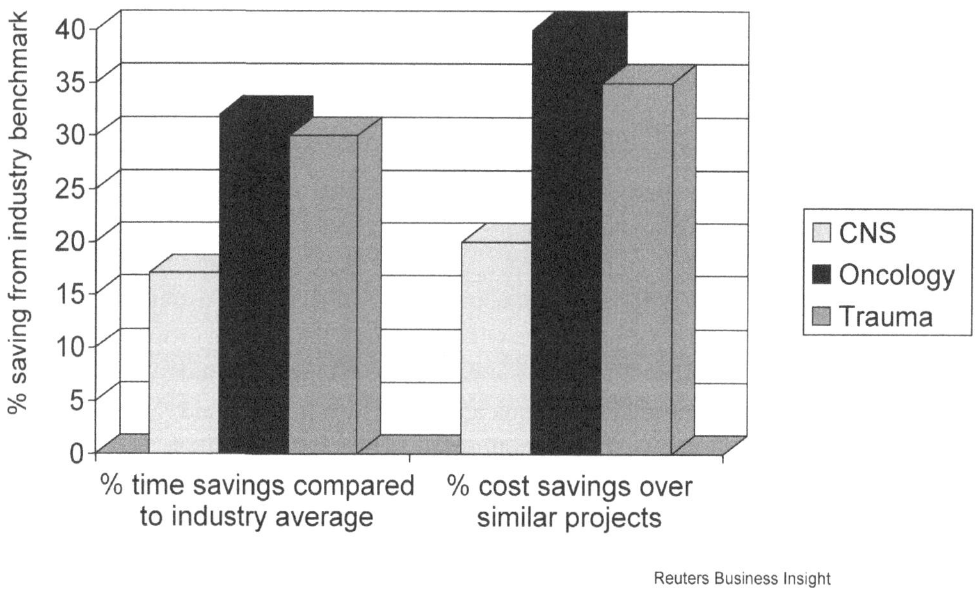

Figure 1.9 Cost savings achieved through a virtual development approach
Source: Fulcrum

The common strategy of these companies is to in-license drugs, increase value and sell on. In principle, their greatest contribution should be their ability to lower cost through focused development so that small and niche products become profitable. Such a service has value as these products are often commonly overlooked by larger pharma companies because of the demanding financial returns they expect from their R&D investment. However, the question remains whether the emphasis on developing products in areas with unmet medical needs will ever gather momentum.

STRATEGIC OUTSOURCING – A ROAD TRAVELLED

Is strategic outsourcing a contradiction of terms considering the current state of play within the pharmaceutical industry? The answer is probably a cautious 'Yes'. As discussed, the majority of pharma companies tend to view and associate outsourcing with procurement. A tactical solution to a short-term tactical problem, outsourcing is often perceived to be an increasingly important but nonetheless necessary evil which allows resources to be secured at the lowest possible price:

- A means by which a company can manage the erratic and often difficult-to-forecast workflow in drug development.
- A means through which the increasing dependence of companies on in-licensed products for development can be managed and to off-set low levels of in-house productivity.

In other industries outsourcing has become so sophisticated that most functions can, and are, outsourced. This in turn has changed the way companies think about their organisations, their value chains and competitive positions. In the pharmaceutical industry, it is clear that in order to increase the value of development pipelines, pharma companies need to make their development value chains and development organisations more flexible.

For more mature outsourcing industries, sourcing is evolving into a strategic process for organising and fine-tuning corporate value chains (Gottfredson, Puryear and Phillips, 2005). The question for pharma is no longer whether, but *how* to source every single activity in the value chain? Greater focus on capability sourcing can improve a company's strategic position by speeding up development, improving quality and reducing costs. Finding more qualified partners to provide critical functions allows companies to enhance the core capabilities that drive competitive advantage. Pharmaceutical companies should move away from seeing clinical development as a strategic capability and therefore keeping all elements within their organisation.

So how can pharmaceutical companies come up with a strategic approach to sourcing in clinical development? Gottfredson, Puryear and Phillips (2005) have developed an elegant model applicable to the clinical development value chain. The first step is to identify the components of clinical development that a pharma company does more cost effectively than the competition. Typical examples include study start-up, patient recruitment and interaction with drug regulatory authorities. In deciding what to outsource, one needs to assign a proprietary value to a process or function and a degree of commonality. By plotting each of the required capabilities on a sourcing opportunities map, one can judge the relation merits of the outsourcing possibilities (Figure 1.10). The vertical axis measures how proprietary a capability is for a company. The horizontal axis plots how common the capability is within or outside the industry. Capabilities that fall in the upper right portion of the map are strong candidates for outsourcing. If pharmaceutical companies would undertake such an exercise they would quickly come to the conclusion that the majority of clinical development activities could be outsourced.

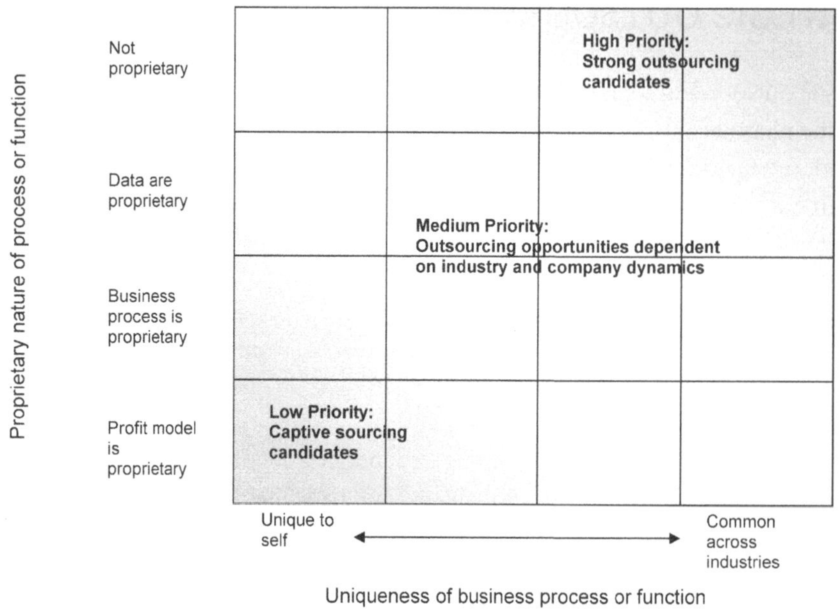

Figure 1.10 Sourcing opportunities map (with permission from Harvard Business School)

The next question is how cost-effectively the company currently performs each of the capabilities that offer the highest potential value from outsourcing (Figure 1.11). One of the difficulties with populating this map for clinical development is the lack of proper and benchmarked cost information. Very often the available clinical development costs only reflect compensation cost and operational expenditure, but neglect the overhead costs

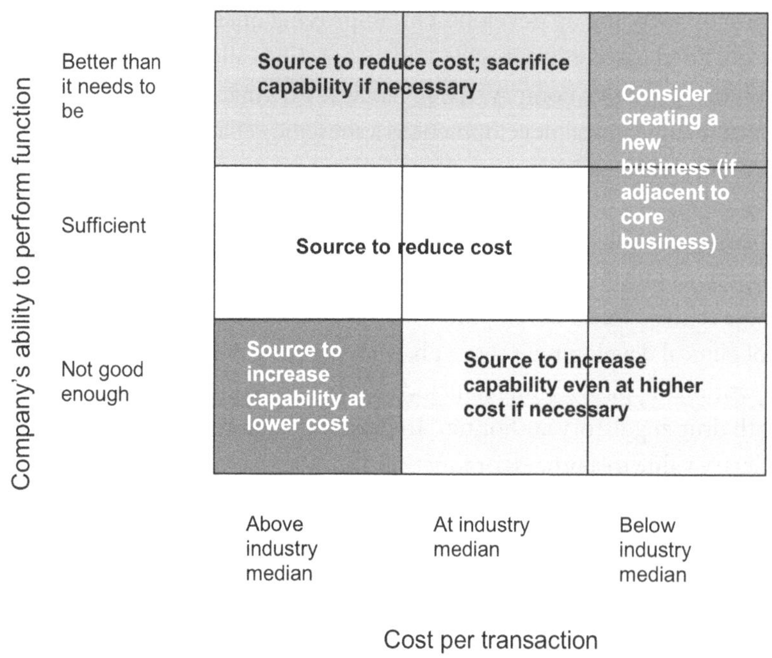

Figure 1.11 Capability assessment map (with permission from Harvard Business School)

which are usually carried centrally. Functions that fall in the upper and lower left require outsourcing partners with a different focus on quality and costs.

Gottfredson, Puryear and Phillips are adding a third step, a reality check. In clinical development that could be the need to have close contacts with KOLs and the medical community at large. Unfortunately, this reality check is very often used to decide against outsourcing in clinical development. Such a decision overlooks the fact that there are more effective ways of working with KOLs. In addition, in this era of cost containment, the influence of KOLs on prescribing patterns will diminish.

By following this three-step approach, it seems pharma should be able to come up with a strategic view of capability sourcing in clinical development. A handful of established pharma companies have come to the same outcome without following this approach, partly out of necessity and partly by vision.

Strategic outsourcing – a competitive asset

To move forward, and for real value to be realised, strategic outsourcing can no longer be viewed as a financially material, yet strategically peripheral, corporate function. Rather it needs to be moved centre-stage, and its leverage viewed as a competitive asset in an increasingly competitive environment. Real derived value, which is clearly and closely aligned with the long-term strategic goals of both the pharma company and CRO, need to be identified, quantified and translated into operational delivery.

In so doing, the term strategic outsourcing will transcend the current sequential and step-wise changes in outsourcing relationships. It will no longer be seen as the end game in a sequence of events. Rather the term will become synonymous with the means by which outsourcing can affect *profound change* within a sponsor organisation, an underlying tenet which could affect all of the steps in a traditional outsourcing continuum.

Achieving this will pose challenges for all players. Changes in attitudes, behaviour and ways of working will be essential critical factors within both the pharma and CRO market sectors if each is to enjoy the benefits that strategic outsourcing could play in their corporate futures.

The pharmaceutical industry challenge

The next decade is predicted to be one of unprecedented pressure upon the global pharmaceutical industry. The large pharma companies will feel this in particular, as expectations for their performance runs towards double-digit growth. Within the current economic and drug development environment, large pharma will need to launch two products a year to deliver 5 per cent annual growth, five products a year to deliver 10 per cent growth and nine products a year to achieve 15 per cent annual growth.

To meet these expectations, pharma companies, like companies in other sectors before them, will have to radically re-evaluate their business model. Specifically they will have to ruthlessly assess and classify their businesses into core and non-core areas, as well as facilitate trust and delegation as part of a new way of working with their outsourced partners.

The traditional value-chain within pharma companies, established and operated successfully for the last 20–30 years, no longer suits. Where once the wholly asset-owned model of vertical integration encompassing research, discovery, development, manufacture, sales and marketing, plus distribution, proved efficient, today this is no longer the case. Globalisation and technology innovation, coupled with the notorious risk-base in pharmaceutical drug development where only two out of every 30 drugs developed will launch, have served to challenge existing definitions of competitive advantage.

That notwithstanding, challenging a hitherto extremely successful business model requires determination and ruthless application. It will undoubtedly encounter resistance as the process will challenge deep-seated beliefs. For the pharmaceutical industry, many of these revolve around two core questions:

- What is the intellectual property of the organisation?
- What confers competitive advantage?

Ownership of all the capabilities or processes that form part of a company's output is no longer the optimum business model, particularly in a global industry. Pharmaceutical executives are realising that true and agile competitiveness is achieved as much by the ability to effectively manage non-core capabilities as identifying and successfully managing core capabilities.

Assessing core and non-core business

The biggest and most difficult challenge facing pharma companies is thus to ruthlessly define their core capabilities. For some this path will lead them to view hitherto sacrosanct, core activities as non-core. Activities such as drug development where global leverage and cost-efficient regulatory, data management and study monitoring skills are important, could be re-defined thus. This was the view Solvay Pharmaceuticals came to in 1998 prior to their innovative and ground-breaking strategic outsourcing partnership deal with Quintiles Transnational. It was also the view that Wyeth Pharmaceuticals came to in 2003 with their equally innovative agreement with Accenture Limited, within which their entire data management capability was defined as non-core, and outsourced accordingly.

In each of the above, the decision to strategically outsource has potentially had a *profound impact* upon their business. For Wyeth, the initial objective was to ultimately enable the data entry function to be implemented at 50 per cent of the costs previously incurred by the company. Interim public reports of the outsourcing performance suggest that key milestones have been achieved and that the initial objective is on track towards being realised (Accenture, 2005).

For Solvay Pharmaceuticals, the strategic outsourcing partnership has resulted in true pipeline enhancement for two of its pivotal development products. Development timelines have been substantially reduced and the potential of shorter time-to-market, with all the attendant additional sales benefit, is evident.

For others, the core and non-core evaluation will result in their assessment of every capability within their organisation, identifying whether they are best-in-class in that function against comparative industry standards. A negative answer should confer the possibility, and arguably a business-robust rationale, for consideration of outsourcing that capability.

Understanding pharma core competencies and resource planning

Alexander and Young (1996) have suggested that there are four meanings associated with core competency. They are:

- activities traditionally performed in-house;
- activities critical to business performance;
- activities creating current or potential competitive advantage; and
- activities that will drive future growth, innovation or rejuvenation.

None of these definitions are really ideal and on the basis of this most pharma companies would outsource nothing in clinical development. Hamel and Prahalad (1994) have presented a new framework for core competencies, arguing that it should be defined in terms of intellectual and knowledge-based service capabilities. These competencies should be more enduring than the products currently produced and be the platform from which the company may successfully develop products of the future. However, Domberger (1998) has argued that identifying core competencies does not provide a sound basis for outsourcing decisions. Domberger proposes that a more appropriate basis on which to make an outsourcing decision is that of specialisation, and hence relative efficiency. A potentially useful way of deciding what to outsource in clinical development could be the use of a sourcing opportunities map as outlined earlier. The two maps proposed by Gottfredson, Puryear and Phillips (2005) could thus be modified for clinical development, as shown in Figures 1.12 and 1.13.

By completing these two maps, a pharma company is able to identify the capabilities offering the highest potential value from outsourcing. The next step is for the pharma company to decide whether it wants to outsource these capabilities. Factors to be considered could include, for example, that they do not wish to outsource the start-up process because the involvement of the local affiliate will be needed for regulatory submissions and that splitting the task in two would derail the seamless process that is needed.

Other factors include acknowledging and understanding how best to successfully work with outsourcing partners. Legacy master-slave notions will have to be put aside in favour of genuine discussion and debate around mutual corporate *modus operandi* that enables a

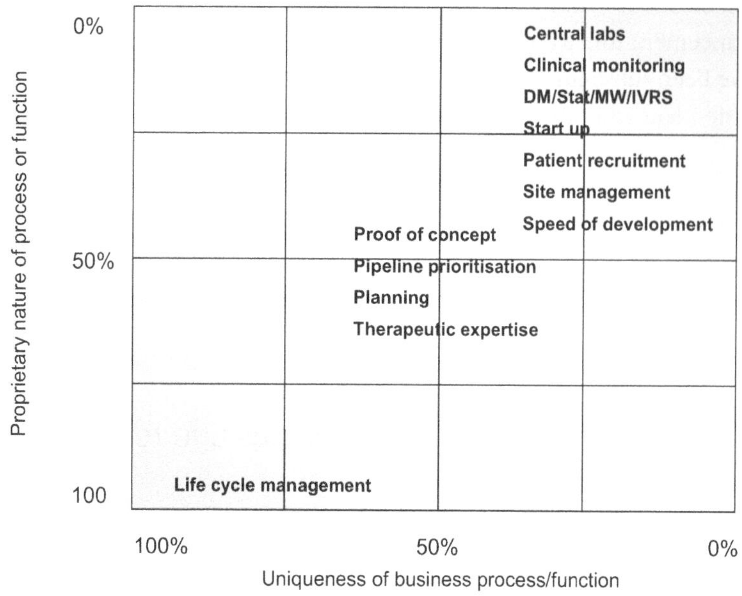

Figure 1.12 Sourcing opportunities map for clinical development

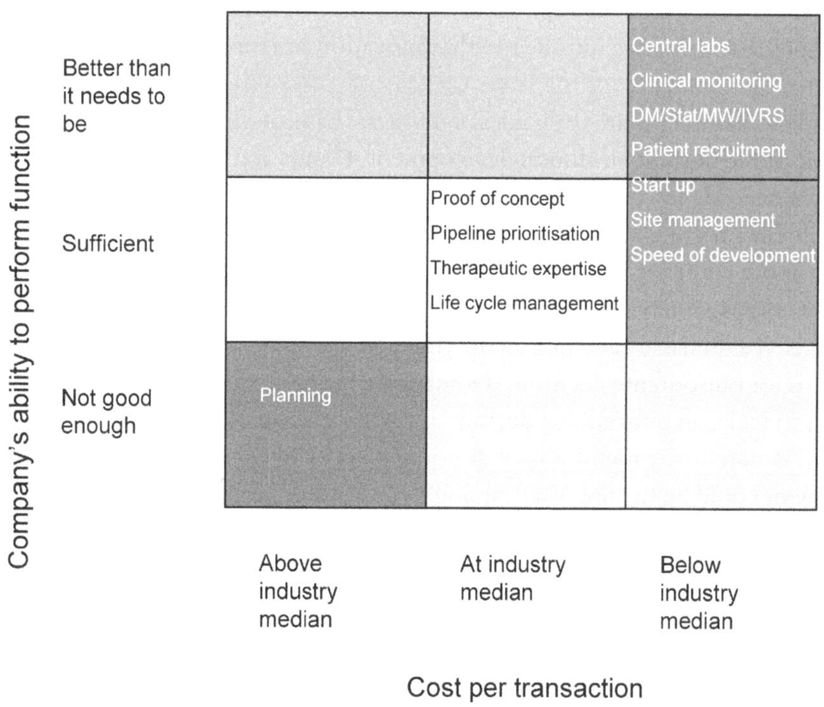

Figure 1.13 Capability assessment map for clinical development

win-win outcome for both parties involved. Trust and delegation will have to be practised as well as mooted.

For the pharma industry this will essentially boil down to relinquishing their perceived control over parts of the drug development process. That control, as currently exercised, results in the paradoxical situation that as many people may be employed to watch and control a CRO as are employed in the CRO for the specific purpose of effectively and efficiently delivering a quality output. From a cost-efficiency stand-point such a practice clearly cannot continue.

Nevertheless, quantifying the cost of CRO management is a thorny subject within the industry. Indeed a whole employee sector has been created to manage CROs – contracts, outsourcing and procurement personnel – not to mention duplication within clinical development personnel. A few brave souls have articulated that the CRO management cost is probably within 15–30 per cent of the costs for an average phase II–III study, but whatever the true cost, it is clear that the need for supervision at this level flies in the face of the principle of partnership and trust, pre-requisites of strategic outsourcing designed to impart a profound effect upon the success of an organisation.

CRO industry challenges

Conceived about 20 years ago, today's CRO has evolved from being a pure capability and capacity outsourcing option, to one where an increasing percentage of the pharma company client base are entering into PPAs. The basis for this evolution in outsourcing type is, however, still based on the core need to cut costs and induce maximum efficiencies from the drug development process.

Strategic outsourcing examples whereby a profound effect upon a sponsor's business has been achieved are few and far between, although there is evidence of an increasing number of opportunities for such discussions to be initiated and undertaken.

Strategic outsourcing which affects a profound impact upon a sponsor's business should be the goal of the CRO industry. To achieve this, the CRO industry faces its own challenges, the key three of which are:

- demonstrating clear value to enhance a client's development productivity;
- assisting creation of outsourcing strategies which deliver, and profoundly impact upon a company's business;
- accepting risk.

Demonstrating clear value – enhance development productivity

Simply performing tasks more effectively will not in itself deliver continuous enhanced productivity. CROs must take pride in, and have the confidence to, leverage their significant scientific credentials, to the benefit of their clients. The agile and flatter structures of CROs are themselves conducive to facilitating a wider drug development perspective on a potential problem. CROs are thus uniquely placed to become solution-providers leveraging corporate scientific acumen. As the pharma sector itself reassesses its core and non-core competencies, this broad-based development perspective, applied appropriately, will become a true competitive edge for a CRO.

Applied appropriately this can, and has, resulted in productivity enhancements achieved through superior delivery. Activities that were previously considered and conducted in a sequential pattern can, in such a relationship, be conducted along a continuum (Figure 1.14).

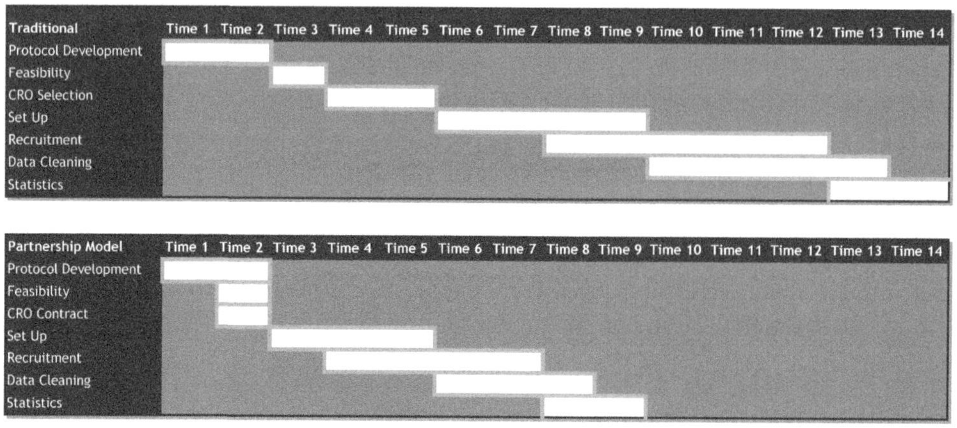

Figure 1.14 Productivity enhancement

Drug development conducted within the framework of a strategic partnership will also be characterised by clear roles and responsibilities with clear lines of communication established from the outset. These, together with clear scope of work and autonomy with regard to patient recruitment and site selection, will result in superior delivery and therein proof of added value.

Achieving a profound impact upon a company's business

Achieving a profound impact upon a customer's business necessitates the development of a strategic outsourcing strategy that is in tune with realisation of the client's goals, and strategically leverages the value of the selected CRO partner.

Developing a true strategic outsourcing strategy such as this will require considerable corporate input, and focus on resistance will be inevitable, challenging as it does, a tried, tested model, operating over at least two decades.

Current outsourcing is done by ex-clinical study managers who honed their skills doing studies in-house. Hence their need for control is high – and is in direct conflict with how to get the best out of an agile, lean and mean structured CRO, focused on 100 per cent utilisation.

Internal shareholder education and awareness should not and cannot be overlooked. Nor should the acknowledgement that developing and maturing a strategic relationship to the point where it can impact a profound benefit to a client organisation, will take time. Ideally a strategic outsourcing strategy should cover a minimum of three and preferably five years. The starting point in its development is company assessment of capabilities and needs.

Among the areas for a pharma company to consider are:

- therapy area expertise

- analysed pipeline and timelines in areas of therapeutic expertise
- in-licensing strategy including therapeutic area and timelines
- type and number of studies needed for each therapy area programme
- number of patients and required countries and/or site location for each therapy area programme, taking into account commercial needs
- resource levels in-house; retention projection and expertise mapping against emerging pipelines
- key critical success factors per suite of studies required and gap analysis conducted with regard to pivotal activities and insource capabilities
- financial framework
- key new drug/product line application dates.

In addition, expectations from the relationship and therein the CRO are essential. Areas to consider here include:

- CRO short list and selection criteria outline
- communication and *modus operandi* plan for CRO working
- minimal duplication of overseeing roles on client side
- specify key success evaluation criteria:
  - *performance* – study performance and cost savings – rates card, unit costs, staff turnover strategy, staff retention policies and so on; clear success milestones
  - *control* – performance milestones and payment schedule linked; bonus/penalty clauses
  - *collaboration* – communication plan; escalation process; governance structure; risk management forum and forecasting.

Accepting risk

Accepting risk in this context of CRO challenges does not refer to risk mitigation by a CRO as part of a contractual arrangement with a preferred partnership or strategic partnership/alliance. Rather, accepting risk here refers to the need for the CRO industry to drive and mobilise the change required in pharmaceutical industry outsourcing.

A great deal of discussion has been set against the inherent trepidation that currently bedevils the pharmaceutical industry. The industry is caught between the rational knowledge that dramatic changes are in order if corporate drug development ambitions are to be realised and the emotional knowledge that the current system has spawned a successful industry. So why meddle with a seemingly perfect and working business model?

The CRO industry is itself maturing into a solutions-based, strategic partner. Senior executives within the CRO industry are aware and excited about the profound impact that the strategic outsourcing can have upon the pharmaceutical industry challenge of mitigating or reducing drug development costs.

This awareness and excitement will need to be mobilised through concrete channels. Pharma executives will need proof if they are to be persuaded to engineer profound and far-reaching changes within their organisations.

This proof represents the risk that the CRO industry needs to acknowledge and accept. The industry will, in all likelihood, need to bear the burden of trust and commitment, and therein corporate risk, in order to enable pharma companies to travel the road towards more strategic outsourcing, capable of impacting profound change and benefit to drug development.

CONCLUSIONS

Outsourcing is now an established part of the drug development process. It has evolved from being used to manage fluctuating capacity needs to its rightful place as part of a company's strategy for addressing their drug development needs.

Strategic outsourcing, however, still remains a concept for the pharma industry. While CROs are stepping up to fulfil the demands of this very specific and special role, the industry has yet to fully embrace its potential benefits. To do so will require pharma companies to ruthlessly evaluate their core and non-core business, accepting that outsourcing can and should be leveraged to be their unforeseen competitive asset.

The CRO industry will need to drive this acceptance of its strategic role, accepting risk and trusting in the long-term benefits that can be enjoyed as the pharma sector slowly adopts strategic outsourcing as a central component of a competitive drug development strategy.

REFERENCES

Accenture (2005) *Experts Share Lessons Learnt: Enabling High Performance Through Outsourcing*. http://www.accenture.com/Global/Services/By_Subject/Business Process_Outsourcing/Customized_Business_Process_Outsourcing/RandI/ DiscoverExperts.htm.

Alexander M. and Young D. (1996) 'Strategic Outsourcing', *Long Range Planning*, **29**(1), pp. 116–19.

Bowden M. and MacKenzie-Lawrie S. (2002) 'Looking at the Next Generation of CROs', *Scrip Magazine*, March 2002, pp. 36–37.

Domberger S. (1998) *The Contracting Organisation: A Strategic Guide to Outsourcing*, Oxford: Oxford University Press.

Drtina R.E. (1994) 'The Outsourcing Decision', *Management Accounting*, March 1994, pp. 56–62.

Eroglin D. (1994), 'Global or Domestic Outsourcing of the "IS" Function: Implications and Recommendations', in Zahra S.A. and Ali A. (eds) *The Impact of Innovation and Technology in the Global Marketplace*, New York: International Business Press.

Goldman Sachs (2004) 'A New Global Pharma Outsourcing Market Model to 2007' in *Parexel's Pharmaceutical R&D Statistical Sourcebook 2004/2005*, Waltham, MA: Parexel International, pp. 26–29.

Goldman Sachs (2000, 2003) *Pharmaceutical Outsourcing*.

Gottfredson M., Puryear R. and Phillips S. (2005) 'Strategic Sourcing: From Periphery to the Core', *Harvard Business Review*, Feb., pp. 1–9.
Hamel G. and Prahalad C.K. (1994) *Competing for the Future*, Boston: Harvard University Press.
King S. and Cuddigan M. (2003) 'Where Next for CROs?', *Scrip Magazine*, Sept., pp. 56–57.
Lacey K. (2003) 'Outsourcing: The New Strategic Tool', *Scrip Magazine*, Dec., pp. 30–31.
Law J. (2004) 'The Reductionist Approach', *Scrip Magazine*, June, pp. 55–58.
McHugh P., Merlin G. and Wheeler W.A. (1995) *Beyond Business Process Re-engineering*, Chichester: John Wiley.
Quinn J.B. (1992) *Intelligent Enterprise: A Knowledge and Service Based Paradigm for Industry*, New York: Free Press.
Quintiles/Innovex Survey (2003) *Outsourcing within the Pharmaceutical Industry*. Research conducted by Insight Research Group.
'Sponsors Send Mixed Message to CROs', *CenterWatch*, Feb. 1998, pp. 4–12.
Walker G. and Weber D. (1984) 'A Transaction Cost Approach to Make-or-Buy Decisions', *Administrative Science Quarterly*, **29**, pp. 373–91.

CHAPTER 2

Selection of Candidates

Rikke Winther, *H. Lundbeck A/S*

Due to increasingly restrictive regulatory requirements, the processes of drug development and obtaining drug approvals have become more lengthy and complex during the past ten years. In order to meet the needs for higher productivity, quality outcome and shortening of timelines, outsourcing to contract research organisations (CROs) is today an important element of most sponsor drug development strategies.

Sponsors adopt varying strategies when deciding which types of activities to outsource in order to meet their specific requirements. Their needs may include anything from short-term usage of a few CRO resources (often referred to as 'tactical outsourcing') to long-term 'strategic outsourcing' as described in more detail in Chapter 8.

As complexity of clinical drug development increases and demands for compliance grow, so the time, efforts and skills required to select the best CRO for any type of work becomes increasingly more critical in the outsourcing process. From a compliance perspective, it is important to have internal procedures to ensure that the selection criteria are documented together with the evaluation of CROs against these criteria and to demonstrate that the CRO was appropriate to deliver the services outsourced.

The processes described in this chapter will focus on the selection of CROs in tactical and study-specific outsourcing, that is, from the point where the decision to outsource a well-defined set of tasks has been made to the point where suitable CROs have been identified from a larger pool of candidate CROs.

The following points need to be considered in the process of selecting candidate CROs, and will be dealt with in detail in this chapter:

- Defining the tasks to be outsourced, timeline for the selection process, and the team to conduct the CRO selection

- Specifying the CRO capabilities that are critical for performing the tasks
- Identifying CROs that possess such capabilities
- Preparing and submitting Request for Information (RFIs) to short-listed candidates and analysing responses
- Retrieving further information
- Final selection of CROs to receive the Request for Proposal (RFP) as further described in Chapter 3.

SPECIFYING TASKS, THE TEAM AND THE TIMELINES

Choosing an outsourcing vendor is like picking a spouse. You can search a long time, but the right partner ultimately is the one you can trust.[1]

Needless to say, sponsors need to be able to clearly define the detailed scope of work and quality standards expected in order to ensure that any selected CRO performs accordingly. This needs careful planning, with appropriately experienced people in the outsourcing team. Internal budgets should be defined and, last but not the least, a process of defining responsibilities, timelines, expectations and milestones should be established as early as possible. Even though this step in the process is critical for successful outsourcing, it is often given a low priority or even ignored for various reasons such as late decisions to outsource or shortened timelines in the study conduct and completion.

From the very beginning, identifying the right people to be involved in the selection process is crucial for defining the tasks to be outsourced, evaluating options and finally in making the right decisions. The size and composition of the people in the outsourcing team may vary, depending on what types of activities are to be outsourced, and at which level the sponsor will be managing and overseeing the CRO, once the activities are conducted. Outsourcing an entire function, such as the data management function of an entire organisation, or a full study, from protocol design through to clinical study report, takes a higher level of commitment and time for the outsourcing team than if outsourcing is limited to single services for a study, such as performing biometrics for a single study only.

The level of sponsor involvement in the entire outsourcing process tends to be higher for larger pharmaceutical companies with a well-defined CRO management group and clinical research resources compared to smaller biotech companies, for example with more limited resources. The latter is more likely to depend on the CRO's capabilities, locations and scientific or technical expertise, whereas a larger organisation would usually have its own experienced resources and locations involved. For both small and large teams, the appropriate level of expertise should be considered as part of the core team or their skills called upon when required. Skills to consider in an outsourcing team include:

- Operational expertise as appropriate to the services being outsourced, including project management
- Technical skills, for example IT, laboratory, pharmacokinetics, therapeutic area

1. Baldo, A. (2004) *Outsourcing Essentials*, **2**(2).

- People management skills
- Outsourcing and negotiations expertise
- Legal skills
- Financial skills.

Setting the timelines of the selection process will again vary depending on the project critical path, scope of the outsourcing activities and when the activities should be initiated at the selected CRO. As a guideline, the timelines of the following elements should as a minimum be clearly understood and agreed by the sponsor team during the start-up phase of the outsourcing initiative:

- Study outline available
- Definitions of scope of work for the CRO
- CRO capability requirements
- Identification of potential candidates
- Initial preselecting of candidates
- Submission of RFI (where appropriate)
- Submission of RFP
- Collection and evaluation of proposals
- Meetings with and/or visits to final short-listed two to three CRO candidates, often termed 'bid-defence' meetings (see Chapter 3)
- Final selection of CRO
- Meeting with CRO defining and confirming details of scope of work, timelines and so on
- Negotiations of prices, legal terms, and so on – depending on the importance of price, this step may come before the final selection of CROs
- Contract approved and work orders/specifications work sheets signed off.

This chapter will address the first six of these points, with the following seven covered in detail in Chapter 3.

SPECIFYING THE CRITICAL CRO CAPABILITIES

The starting point is ideally when the scope of work, objectives, expectations, timelines, geographical locations and so on, are defined. However, this is not always possible and as a minimum the sponsor should have an outline scope and objectives for the project in order to understand the CRO capabilities they will be looking for.

The next step is to prepare the CRO capabilities checklist. This is usually prepared by the contracts manager, outsourcing team or project manager. The checklist could as a minimum include:

- study requirements and thereby the service capabilities required: for example full service, biometrics, monitoring only;
- geographies required;
- resources;

- experience and capabilities needed, both in terms of personnel and therapeutic area;
- approach and need of project management;
- ability to meet specific project objectives.

In addition, the effort taken to prepare response, communication and adherence to the timelines should be considered.

The next stage of the process is to begin looking for the CROs which mostly closely match those requirements identified in the CRO capabilities checklist. A checklist should be completed for each CRO considered and particularly for those on the potential shortlist, and taken to the next stage.

The CRO market

The CRO market can basically be divided into four broad categories:

1. Global commodity full service CROs offering a global service, that is, those CROs present in major countries and offering 'one-stop-shopping' services from pre-clinical through to marketing. A number of such CROs are headquartered in the United States, Europe and Asia/Pacific.

2. Full service CROs typically based in a region such as the US, Europe or Asia and offering full service capabilities within that region.

3. Local specialty CROs offering a limited range of services, either with respect to location or expertise. Thus, these CROs tend to operate in a single country or are only offering services within a few disciplines or niches. They may have expertise in specific therapeutic areas or offer specific phase I capabilities, interactive voice response system services or cardiac services. All major clinical research markets have local CROs who offer site selection, monitoring and project management. More specialist services such as phase I, data management and statistics can be offered either through internal expertise or partnerships with other CROs or universities.

4. Global specialty CROs (or niche CROs) which offer services within a niche discipline. Their capabilities may be defined by geographical, therapeutic or methodological expertise making them unique in the CRO market.

There is no clear guideline as to which type of CRO fits best with a small versus a large pharma organisation, and starting to investigate the variety of CRO capabilities can quickly become an exhaustive exercise. Generally, the smaller companies often look for the more flexible and personal approach, where they may be given higher priority. They may feel that this is best offered by CROs of a similar size, where they are not competing with the much larger business of multi-national pharmaceutical companies. Due to very scarce resources, there seems to be a tendency for smaller biotech companies to select the global commodity CROs which can offer the full range of services needed in the early development phases as well as the geographical spread required for the later phase studies. However, some biotech companies are very specialised and targeted within their field of therapeutic expertise, and they may prefer to work with global speciality (niche) CROs.

Mid-size pharma companies tend to be attracted to mid-size CROs – often based on best match on company cultures being alike. In contrast, large pharma companies appear to work across the entire spectrum of CROs and often enter into long-term preferred provider relationships or even partnerships with a few selected CROs.

It is hard to generalise as to when to use a particular type of CRO, but some ideas are provided in Table 2.1.

Table 2.1 Suggested use of CROs

Activities to be outsourced	Global commodity full service CRO	Full service CRO	Global speciality CROs	Local speciality CROs
Clinical development programme				
Phase I				
Phase II and III				
Multi-centre, specialist trail, for example oncology				
Multi-centre specialist trail, for example specific region				

Defining CRO capabilities within a particular outsourcing situation is often a mix of elements and again will be valued differently from one company to another. The more obvious elements are detailed below:

- Organisational size and structure
- Operational expertise and experience
- Therapeutic or methodological expertise
- Geographical location(s)
- Costs and financial stability
- Risk-sharing opportunities.

However, it is important not to forget the more 'soft' capabilities such as:

- Adaptation/understanding of sponsor requirements
- Flexibility
- Cultural fit (compatibility between sponsor and CRO operations and management)
- Reputation

- Willingness to go the extra mile, and so on
- Rapport between project managers and team in each of the stakeholders.

IDENTIFYING CROS

Once the tasks and the critical capabilities are clearly defined and the selection process is well understood by the sponsor team, the search for suitable candidates can commence. As explained above, the search criteria must reflect the nature of the sponsor organisation. Thus these criteria will differ for a biotech sponsor with limited internal resources to manage the CRO, compared to a larger sponsor with its own expertise and management resources.

For smaller biotech sponsors, internal resources to control and manage the selection process may not be available and therefore external consultants or companies specialised in providing these services could become involved at this stage. They would be expected to follow the same process as described below.

The following list is not exhaustive, but will serve as a guideline for commencing the search, assessing the information that is publicly available, known by sponsor's experience or recommended by others.

Past experience

Internal past experience can be invaluable to assess how a future relationship with a CRO will work. It is recommended that details of how successful a relationship – or not successful, as the case may be – are recorded. This is important to improve outsourcing relationships going forward. Other ideas include:

- By sponsor or by individual sponsor employees having past experience: valuable information could be gathered by submission of questionnaires to relevant functions/regions or employees at sponsor.

- From preferred provider lists already established by sponsor.

- By referring to lessons learnt information captured by the project teams on a previous project.

- From CRO relationship managers in larger sponsor companies.

Although it is important to capture experience gained from previous relationships, care has to be taken in the type of information that is recorded about either a company or individuals. Consideration should be given to the Data Protection Act, local guidance and legislation applicable to that country to ensure that non-compliance is avoided.

Recommendation

Recommendations from other sources are beneficial when considering a CRO, which is unknown to the sponsor. Ideas to be considered here include:

- From external colleagues in the industry, for example from other sponsors already conducting work with the CRO.

- From consultants, for example specialists in providing sponsors with services within CRO benchmarking, such as fast track systems.

- Through networking in the industry, for example, the Pharmaceutical Contract Management Group (PCMG) in Europe or the Pharmaceutical Outsourcing Management Association (POMA) in the US.

Internet

The Internet can be a valuable reference to identify suppliers and understand their capabilities. Sources include:

- Databases, for example Pharmsource, Technomark, Center Watch, DrugDev123, Pharmaceutical Online, Drug Information Association (DIA)
- CRO's own web pages
- Publications on the web (see also below)
- eMarket organisations.

Publications

Publications may carry articles, features, advertisements or advertorials and may be divided into four main types:

- Specialist guides, for example those published by Technomark, Pharmafile, and so on
- Trade publications, for example *Contract Pharma*, *Chemistry Today*, *Pharmaceutical Technology Europe*, *Scrip*, and so on
- Professional journals, for example *Applied Clinical Trials*
- General journals, for example *Journal of the British Institute of Regulatory Affairs*.

Meetings, conferences and training courses

Commercial organisations hold specialist meetings, conferences and training courses on outsourcing in the UK, in mainland Europe and the US; these include:

- Management Forum, PCMG, IIR or ICM. These companies often advertise meetings, training courses and conferences in the field of outsourcing.

- CROs regularly attend, present and exhibit at conferences such as IIR – Annual Partnerships Conference, DIA or Annual Institute of Clinical Research (ICR) conference.

Cold calls and mail shots

Most CROs employ business development managers to actively promote their services. These CRO representatives are able to explain their company's capabilities and how they could assist the sponsor. The business development managers can also provide further information via:

- brochures, publicity handouts, list of references from other sponsors that the CRO has previously worked with or is currently working with;

- detailed lists of current CRO expertise within the service to be outsourced, for example list of services or studies performed, list of therapeutic area expertise, list of available relevant CRO staff, locations and so on.

Using the information to pre-select the CROs

The above sources of identification should aim towards pre-selecting the most suitable number of candidates that appear to have the right capabilities. The number of candidates would for one company be five to ten – for another the list of candidates could be much smaller. The next stage in the CRO selection process in some companies is to send out a Request for Information (RFI). However, in other sponsor companies the next step is to send out a Request for Proposal (RFP), which is dealt with in Chapter 3. The need for a RFI may depend on whether:

- there is a corporate requirement
- the amount of information available on the cro is sufficient
- the size of project and the associated risk
- the scope of the outsourcing strategy.

PREPARING AND SUBMITTING RFI AND ANALYSING RESPONSES

Using a RFI enables the sponsor to gather a broad range of information on potential CROs. The information is more general than that sought from a RFP, and can be used to evaluate capabilities and experience, before understanding how a specific project could be delivered. Having identified the CROs to receive the RFI, the evaluation of the responses may enable a further narrowing down of the number of CROs to three to five, which would be considered for the next step in the selection process, receipt of the RFP, as described in Chapter 3.

THE RFI

The nature of this request and accompanying documentation varies between companies, and may depend on company policy, the service required (for example much more detailed information than is included below would be requested as part of the process for selection of a preferred provider where the risk is greater), size and scale of project, time available to the selection team, and so on.

For example, company procedure may not require that a confidentiality agreement is in place beforehand, as minimal information regarding the study will be provided at this stage. Alternatively, some companies may prefer to put a confidentiality agreement in place prior to distribution of the RFI, in order that more specific information about the CRO's experience in that particular therapeutic area can be obtained, and specific questions concerning the planned study can be addressed. By way of general guidance, the format of the RFI might contain some or all of the sections outlined below.

General introduction

The purpose and objective of the RFI would be defined, together with the timelines for completion, and details of whom to contact at the sponsor with questions. Alternatively, this information might be included in a covering letter/email.

Background to study

Information relating to the therapeutic area, generalised mode of action, summary of study design, might be provided in order to focus the CRO's response. Similarly, specific questions relating to the CRO's experience in that therapeutic area/product type/service might be provided, as might information regarding a potential recruitment strategy. Information collected at this stage in the selection process often gives a hint to the sponsor as to the amount of thought, effort and actual experience of the CRO, as well as avenues to be further explored at the RFP stage.

Corporate financial information

It is particularly important to conduct due diligence to ensure that the CRO is financially viable and stable, with a strong balance sheet and cash flow. Although in the current climate of acquisitions and mergers there are no guarantees, but certain considerations should be taken into account:

- Number of years in business and growth of business
- Availability of full financial information; request a copy of the CRO's annual report. Wherever possible, this should be reviewed by an accountant or someone with the appropriate financial training

- Openness to financial analysis, when not publicly traded
- Financial relationship with parent organisation (if applicable), for example, smaller affiliates, phase I units, laboratories and so on can be sold off by parent company
- Business volume; number of projects, size and status
- Number of clients (current vs. cumulative) and revenue share (percentage of work from one or two clients). Similarly, for smaller organisations with fewer clients, if one large project is the major revenue earner, then there is risk in that the stability of the organisation could be compromised if that project/client was lost
- Percentage of repeat business. However, for CROs specifically dealing with smaller clients or early phase work, these figures can be misleading due to the high attrition rate of investigational products.

CRO locations

The location of head office, affiliates and locations of legal entities is an important consideration in terms of anticipated location of study, company culture, and communications. For early phase studies, for example, phase I, where the sponsor may prefer to conduct the study monitoring, accessibility to that clinic/ease of travel can be an important consideration. Similarly, geographical coverage can play a key role in selection of the CRO.

Partnerships (with other CROs and academic institutions)

Very few CROs will offer a completely global service, with representation in each country of interest and able to supply all specialist services required. It is therefore important to carefully question the services offered to determine if they are sub-contracted or outsourced. Even something such as access to patients whether it is direct or via site management organisations or partner CROs should be investigated.

If a service is sub-contracted, the nature of the relationship between CRO/provider should be considered, that is:

- What sort of contract for services exists?
- Who would remain accountable for the service?
- What sort of guarantee does the partner give, in terms of prioritising resource to their partner?

Geographical coverage

Many CROs offer a strategic opportunity to even the large sponsor companies in that their geographical reach is in countries where the sponsor anticipates expanding markets, but as yet does not wish to commit to investment in their own infrastructure. Smaller sponsors, such as biotech, often rely on CROs as 'their hands around the world'. The local knowledge offered by the CROs, of regulatory environment, logistics and access to investigators is often of great benefit to the sponsor.

The areas of coverage are often more important for later phase studies, where the sponsor may be trying to increase awareness of the potential product in key emerging markets. Alternately, patient availability and recruitment potential may provide the focus for location. Depending on the indication, certain countries offer patients naïve to certain treatments, and the centralised health care system can greatly assist access to the appropriate patient populations. For other indications, seasonal requirements may contribute to the preferred location for the study.

Consideration should also be given to the type of coverage offered in the regions represented; for example, does the CRO have a legal entity in that country with office support home-based Clinical Research Associates (CRAs) or is that country monitored from regional CRAs based outside that particular country? All scenarios have their own advantages and disadvantages, and sponsor preference often depends on company outsourcing strategy.

Organisational structure

Details of organisation, for example, global and/or local organograms should be requested. These can give an indication of management structure (for example, hierarchical or matrix), the functionality of each department and of the communication pathways. Depending on the scope of the study, consideration should be given to the communication between head office and affiliate offices and the roles of the equivalent persons in each location. It is often useful for the sponsor to request an example of a project team structure as this can help identify corporate fit between the sponsor and CRO.

Capabilities

There are a number of considerations to be made as regards the CRO's capabilities. One of the most important is whether CROs have the capacity to expand and contract with changing needs and whether they would be capable of taking on the specific project at the time required for the estimated duration.

Depending on the focus of the RFI (general or specific), the level of detail could be left open for the CRO to complete, or the sponsor could indicate the specific services of interest. Such capabilities may include, but are not limited to:

- adeptness at managing compounds across the drug development continuum
- technological and scientific leadership
- protocol development
- feasibility processes
- project management
- site selection, project set up and initiation, monitoring

- data management, statistics
- phase i capability
- pharmacokinetics and pharmacodynamics, and so on
- medical writing
- pharmacovigilance
- pharmacoenconomics
- central laboratories, bioanalysis, and so on
- central electrocardiogran (ECG) services, interactive voice response systems (IVRS) and so on.

Experience

It is extremely important to evaluate whether the CRO has the experience and expertise in the critical area of need. The information requested may be specific to a specific therapeutic area or indication, study design or investigational product (for example, intravenous, biologic, vaccine, and so on). Often the information provided by the CRO is extensive, so therefore it is beneficial to clearly specify the information required, such as type of experience (monitoring, project management, and so on) and in which particular region (Europe, the US and South America, and so on).

It often serves useful to provide a table with headings to be completed so that the information is received back in a uniform format. Suggested headings include (for example, for a specific indication):

- phase of study
- country/countries where the study was performed
- number of centres and patients
- duration of recruitment
- recruitment rate per site or per country
- type of service, for example, monitoring, data management.

The information should be evaluated with caution to differentiate experience from exposure; often experience is accumulated from individuals' past experience, or from past studies, but if all of the team members have since left, the volume of knowledge is reduced. To identify a CRO that has had the actual exposure as a team can be highly advantageous.

Staff

Often it is the quality of the staff and how they are managed that creates a good, reliable organisation which, ultimately, offers a higher probability for the delivery of a successful project. Some of the points to consider include:

- Number of permanent vs. contract staff, full time vs. part time

- Length of time staff have been with the CRO. Specify those of particular interest, for example, medical advisor, project managers, monitors, and so on

- Length of time staff have worked in current role. Again, specify those of interest
- Experience levels of staff. Again, specify those of interest and take as averages when data are presented. A review of individual CVs should be considered here or at the RFP stage
- Attitudes to staff and retainment policies. For example, can the CRO demonstrate investment in their staff; career progression, training, bonus schemes, and so on?
- Management and performance metrics systems
- Management staff turnover and change. Is there sufficient training, adequate handover, back-up personnel? How soon will the sponsor be informed?

Approach to project management

It can prove interesting and useful to obtain an impression of the project management within the organisation. Importantly, does the structure allow for sufficient support, not only within the team, but also from senior management? As project management is one of the key contributors to the success of the project, then the sponsor will need to ensure that the CRO structure is compatible to their own structure – whether organisational or in terms of systems and procedures.

If not at this stage in the selection process, but then the next stage (RFP), a detailed assessment of the approach to risk analysis and contingency planning should be made. Discussion of performance metrics and reporting timelines should be included.

Ultimately, the relationship between the project manager and key project team members with the equivalent members in the sponsor company is critical to the building of a good team and successful project. The personalities, and 'soft' aspects, such as 'Can we work together?' should be carefully explored at the next stage in the selection process.

Quality assurance

As quality is the critical component of all pharmaceutical R&D, it is important to understand the quality systems the CRO has in place, and whether the CRO demonstrates an understanding of, and compliance with, appropriate regulations globally. Some typical questions to be asked include:

- How does the CRO measure quality?
- What processes are in place to continually monitor quality?
- What is the size of the quality assurance (QA) department? Internal or contracted service?
- What internal QA procedures are in place, for example, is it usual for QA to audit studies independent of sponsor-CRO contract, as part of internal CRO quality control?

Recent experience with regulatory inspections may also give an indication of operational quality and regulatory awareness.

Financial processes and reporting

For some sponsors, it may be relevant or even required to investigate whether the CRO financial processes and business procedures are compatible with the sponsor's own procedures and requirements. Some points to be considered may include:

- What is their pricing policy – is there a fixed global rate for activities or is this adjusted regionally?
- Which currency will the contract be in? For lengthy projects, how are currency fluctuations managed?
- Consider flexibility of CRO – what is the attitude towards fixed unit price contracts vs. time and materials, capped budgets vs. penalty or bonus clauses?

Sponsor references

If not already collected earlier in the pre-selection process, it may be useful to request references from other clients of the CRO. However, these references should be interpreted with care as CROs are unlikely to provide all but the best references, thus this may represent a biased source of information. The perception of individual CRO performance is often linked to an individual or team personnel experience. It is often worth trying to seek a wider perspective on potential partners. Hence, just because a CRO performed well for one client in a particular study, or on the other hand performed less well, does not mean that will be the case in the next study; different study designs, study teams (on both the CRO and sponsor side), regulatory climate and commercial pressures can impact on the performance and relationships of both sponsor and CRO.

Miscellaneous

Other points for consideration include but are not limited to:

- If specific projects are held in mind, whether or not the CRO (or their investigators) are working on conflicting studies

- Availability of key, experienced staff, for example, project manager

- For phase I studies, detailed information regarding facilities faculties should be collected, including number of beds, percentage occupancy, location, good manufacturing practice pharmacy, qualified person for packaging/labelling of investigational medicinal product (if required), laboratory facilities, specialist equipment, standard operating procedures (SOPs), and so on

- Methods of speeding up the recruitment process and risk management

- Flexibility and availability.

Ultimately, the choice of CRO should not be down to the hard facts presented alone but should rely on some degree of intuition from the selection team. Openness, realism, responsiveness and the communication experienced throughout the RFI process should contribute significantly in the final selection.

In summary, the RFI should be tailored to the requirements of the sponsor, such as corporate policy and individual study or service requirements. Although in this chapter we have primarily focused on the most appropriate RFI for a CRO being asked to provide classical study management activities, the document should be amended to reflect the specific selection process. Typically, similar sections will be included; however, the emphasis on the relative importance of each section will vary with each project. Table 2.2 gives an example of how criteria would be weighted differently when considering outsourcing a phase I, first dose in man study when compared to a global, phase IV, post-marketing, safety surveillance project.

Table 2.2 Relative weighting of selection criteria by study type

	Phase I	**Phase IV**
Study characteristics		
Study objective	First dose in man	Post-marketing safety surveillance
Subject numbers	Low	High
Number of sites	1 dedicated research site	Large number of unspecialised sites
Volume of data/subject	High	Low
Overall volume of data	Low	High
Complexity	High	Low
Intensity	High	Low
Duration	Short-term	Long-term
Selection criteria to be considered		
Technical and scientific expertise	+++	
Access to key opinion leaders	+	++
Geographical spread		+++
Access to investigators	+	+++
Subject/patient recruitment	++	+++
Project management	++	+++
CRA expertise	++	+
CRA training	++	++
Regulatory knowledge	+	+
Logistical management (for example, drug shipment)	+	+++
Data collection	++	+++
Financial	++	+

GATHERING FURTHER INFORMATION

Towards the final stages of the CRO selection process the capabilities should be well established. For some sponsors or for complex projects with several parties needing to work together (sponsor, one or more CROs, external experts and central laboratories, for example) the interaction and direct communication with the CRO may play an essential role already in this phase of the selection. As sponsor and CRO over time must work together as a team, it is crucial that both parties feel comfortable working together and that processes, expectations and company cultures are well understood. This can be further assessed by:

- Inviting candidates to present their capabilities in person (discussed in Chapter 3). This meeting also provides an opportunity for the sponsor and CRO teams to get a better understanding of the information provided in the RFI responses. It is often useful to ask the candidates to involve both business development staff and operational staff, specifically the project manager proposed for the project.

- Meeting the CROs in their own environment to inspect their facilities, meeting the staff and generally assess the suitability of placing the work. Using a CRA assessment checklist during such a visit will help the sponsor get the most out of the visits, and will also allow the sponsor to compare candidates objectively.

- Conduct pre-selection audits.

- Contact sponsor references following prior acceptance by the CRO.

- Request a review of CROs' Contract and Work Order templates and/or provide sponsor templates to detect fundamental differences in contractual/legal mind-sets, which could lead to time-consuming negotiations or even jeopardising the relationship from the very beginning.

Based on the above assessments, the sponsor should now have a solid foundation and be able to select three or four CRO candidates to go on to receive the detailed RFP and prepare proposals as described in the following chapter.

CHAPTER 3

Request for Proposal

Emma Sabin, *Pfizer Ltd*

The Request for Proposal (RFP) phase of outsourcing often heralds the start of a significant resource requirement for both the sponsor and the potential suppliers. Careful thought and planning in advance can help to minimise the effort required by both parties. It will also maximise the value of the information that is generated for the sponsor. This chapter will consider the two main types of RFP process: sole source (involving one supplier) and competitive tender (where two or more suppliers are approached to provide proposals). It will also consider the key elements of an effective RFP package that will ensure it is tailored and appropriate to the particular outsourcing situation and to meet corporate direction. The final selection of the supplier is also briefly discussed, considering the initial proposal assessment and the merits of utilising a face-to-face meeting versus direct selection by the sponsor on the basis of the proposal documents.

THE AIM OF THE PROCESS

This chapter provides a comprehensive overview of the RFP process. It deals with many of the considerations that are important in working through the RFP process and the degree of consistency required in order to facilitate proposal assessment. These factors are important in enabling the sponsor to make an appropriate decision regarding supplier selection. However, it may be unnecessary to force such a degree of rigidity on the process for some sponsors and/or under some circumstances. It is important to remember that the aim of the RFP process is for the sponsor to obtain an appropriate number of high quality proposals that allow the individual and/or the organisation to make an informed decision regarding the most appropriate supplier to provide the services under consideration. To that end, it is worth taking some time to consider what would be the optimal or even the minimal acceptable outcome from each RFP event and to tailor the request as necessary so that a bespoke response can be solicited that will address these needs. Consistency should not mean lack of thought or planning in advance, and when it comes to the RFP process, one size rarely fits all.

It is also important, in larger sponsor companies, to ensure all functional groups have had time to both provide input into the RFP and review the final document before it is sent out to the short-listed suppliers. This is particularly relevant where the RFP process is being led by a separate contract management group. This increases the quality of the RFP and decreases the chances of significant changes later in the outsourcing process.

CONFIDENTIALITY

Before embarking on any discussions beyond basic capacity and capability investigations with external suppliers, it is essential that appropriate confidentiality agreements be put in place. The agreement can be either one-way (preventing the supplier from using or sharing information provided by the sponsor), or two-way (preventing both the supplier and the sponsor from using or sharing any information that is covered by the agreement). It is all too easy to inadvertently share proprietary information, particularly when discussing the details of an exciting new project with an interested audience. Putting a confidentiality agreement in place at a very early stage, or even covering information shared between the parties at a more generic level (for example, via a clause in a master agreement that covers all dealings between the parties when discussing any project) protects intellectual property and allows free discussion of ideas and concepts between the parties.

INITIAL CONTACT

Once potential companies have been identified, initial contact would normally be made via telephone. Depending on the existing relationship with the supplier (if any), this offers the sponsor an opportunity to begin to gauge the interest of each company, and to give some advanced warning of the detailed information to be expected and the timeframe in which it should be expected. This would then usually be followed up with written details of the project and the sponsor's requirements, and at this stage, the more information that can be provided to the supplier, the better. The secret of a successful RFP is thorough and detailed preparation, both in terms of the approach to be taken and in the RFP package materials. As well as it being a common courtesy to take the time to make an initial call to a potential supplier, it can save time later on.

Inevitably, there is turnover of staff across the industry such that it is worth checking that a previous company contact is still appropriate for the work under consideration. While having a timeframe for response in mind, it is also worth discussing this in person, as it may be possible to prioritise the request with the supplier. Alternatively, other work commitments, training, conference or other conflicting demands may mean that some negotiation of the timeframe is required (if indeed this is possible).

UP-FRONT EFFORT REAPS REWARDS

The quality of the proposal generated by the supplier, and therefore its usefulness to the sponsor, is directly related to the quality of the RFP package. The sponsor clearly has a key role to play in this, and it can often be valuable to assess the RFP process after completion with the aim of continuously improving both the package and the process.

The 'classic' RFP process involves a number of suppliers. Outsourced activities can, however, be 'single sourced' with a proposal being requested from a single supplier, or 'competitively tendered' between two or more suppliers. The general principles for competitive bidding will still apply to sole sourced proposals, although the RFP package of materials and the proposal analysis step may be much simplified.

The basic concept of the RFP is to provide comprehensive and consistent information to suppliers so that it is clear what services are required, by when, how they are to be performed and by whom. The response to the RFP from the suppliers will be the development of a detailed proposal. The key objectives of any proposal are to:

- detail how the services will be delivered;
- identify the resources required; and
- provide a detailed costing.

It is important to obtain high quality proposals for the purposes of supplier selection. In the case of competitive tender, consistent and comprehensive proposals with minimal supplier assumptions are easier to compare on the basis of both service provision and cost. However, other sponsors may be happy to receive the proposal in the supplier format. Even if a single proposal is solicited, accurate and comprehensive information facilitates later negotiation (see Chapter 5) and helps clarify expectations between the parties.

Regardless of how many proposals are involved, the ultimate aim of the RFP process is to select a supplier and eventually to contract with that supplier. The basic scope and assumptions contained in the RFP package drive the information in the proposal, and eventually this information forms the basis for the contract. The clearer and more comprehensive the information at this stage, the easier it is to draft a meaningful contract and the better the basis for managing the contract and any scope changes further down the line. Preparation and up-front thinking saves time later on.

SCOPE OF THE RFP PACKAGE

The scope of the RFP package will depend on what services are to be outsourced and on the selection process that will be employed. For example, if a proposal is required from one supplier for the provision of a simple service that they have provided on a previous occasion (such as medical writing services), the RFP package might only consist of a one-page summary of requirements, combined with a phone call to discuss. Outsourcing of a full service study involving competitive tender among several suppliers may require a number of documents and several discussions with both the manager of the outsourcing process and the project team before a meaningful proposal can be generated.

RFP PACKAGE COMPONENTS

There are a number of components that make up a 'standard' RFP package, and these can be compiled and provided to suppliers in various ways. The standard RFP package typically includes the following:

- protocol synopsis
- scope of services to be delegated
- summary of deliverables
- timelines
- key feasibility questions
- constraints.

The package and the individual components can be varied according to the outsourcing need, but inevitably the more comprehensive the information provided, the more likely it is that the resulting proposal will meet expectations.

Project scope and basic information

The first piece of information to be shared with the potential suppliers is the scope of services that are to be outsourced. The provision of this level of detail is fairly straightforward (for example, data management, patient recruitment or clinical monitoring), and can be used to target the RFP to an appropriate supplier contact. The RFP will require further levels of detail regarding the services to be outsourced, and this will be discussed later in this chapter.

Basic study information that might be contained within a comprehensive RFP package include the protocol or outline protocol synopsis if this is at an early stage of development. Other documents which may be useful if available are the Case Report Form (CRF) and monitoring guidelines.

Other basic information to be provided are the names (telephone numbers and other details, as appropriate) of relevant sponsor contacts, including the person managing the outsourcing event, and potentially the project team members who should be approached with any operational questions arising from the RFP package. An indication of the timelines for the submission of the proposal, the overall selection process and details of the selection mechanism (for example, if a face-to-face meeting will be required) would be useful for the potential suppliers who may need to prioritise the generation of the proposal and ensure the availability of key project staff for a meeting in line with the sponsor's requirements. The sponsor must also decide if the closing date for the submission of proposals is an absolute requirement or is a point for negotiation. Again, it can be useful and save time if this is discussed in person in advance of sending the RFP package to the potential suppliers.

The RFP can be used as a mechanism to start discussion over the terms and conditions that will form an integral part of the contract that is to be generated once the supplier has been selected. However, at this stage, it may be wise to focus only on the non-negotiable or potentially controversial items in order that the process of supplier selection is not unduly affected by discussion of non-key issues. For example, issues such as indemnity and intellectual property will almost certainly require in-depth discussion at a later date.

Assumptions and key cost drivers

As a general rule, assumptions should, wherever possible, be made by the sponsor so that consistent information is given to suppliers. In this way, the costs are generated using the same information and basic premise and the sponsor can compare like-for-like proposals. If the suppliers make their own assumptions, they are highly likely to differ among suppliers, making the job of comparing proposals and selecting a supplier more difficult. If suppliers do make their own assumptions, these must be provided as part of the proposal so that they can be assessed by the sponsor. If the supplier disagrees with the assumptions that are provided (for example, in their experience recruitment rates may be significantly different from that assumed by the sponsor), this should be flagged, but not changed in the base proposal. If a supplier is able to provide a comprehensive alternative scenario that, based on experience, they believe will offer benefits to the sponsor, for example, if the study would be more effective if run in a different group of countries, then they too should be provided. The supplier can either provide alternative scenario proposals or provide details in the same proposal with separate costings provided for each scenario. In this way, the sponsor is still able to compare like-for-like with other supplier proposals, while also assessing the alternative scenarios for feasibility.

The service information that should be provided will depend on the services to be outsourced. It might include:

- number of patients to be recruited
- countries to be used/not to be used
- number of sites
- location of proposed sites (or an assumption of the potential location of sites)
- number of crf pages
- number of monitoring visits.

Qualitative description of monitoring visits can be further broken down into time required on site, travel time and preparation/follow-up time, and again these assumptions can either be detailed up front by the sponsor, or the supplier can be asked to outline their assessment in the proposal for comparison purposes. There are some benefits to this requirement being driven by the sponsor (as a direct comparison can be made between proposals), but there are also benefits to be gained from the supplier being allowed to make their own assumptions where this (and other) key cost drivers are concerned.

Information and assumptions surrounding monitoring visits represent a key cost driver when outsourcing clinical monitoring services. This is because the time involved in monitoring, and therefore the costs associated with this item within the proposal, are one of the main activity items to be considered in this proposal type. If the hours that comprise a monitoring visit and the cost per hour is fixed, together with the number of visits, then there is very little room for manoeuvre on cost. If the assumptions around this are fixed by the sponsor then the supplier has little room to propose the most cost-effective proposal for monitoring.

Other outsourced services will have other key cost drivers, and monitoring visit totals and breakdowns will not be the only cost driver for clinical monitoring. It is important that both the sponsor and the supplier understand what key cost drivers are in operation when outsourcing as they offer an opportunity to manage the proposal costs. The question of consistency for proposal comparison purposes versus flexibility to allow the supplier to provide tailored and cost-effective proposals should be addressed in advance of generating the RFP.

Milestones

Key milestones and expected timelines should be defined, and the supplier given the opportunity to comment on these as they will eventually form part of the contract. Examples of common milestones used in outsourcing are:

- protocol approved
- first site initiated
- last patient recruited
- database locked
- clinical study report approved.

In most cases there will be some degree of flexibility in some or all of these parameters, and there should be the opportunity for these to be discussed. However, any non-negotiable milestones should be clearly identified.

It may be appropriate for the supplier to offer alternative timelines if they believe that either those proposed are not feasible, or perhaps that they can improve on them using an alternative scenario. The sponsor should pay special attention to the feasibility assessment around these key milestones and may wish to flag this expectation up front in the RFP.

Key milestones that are non-negotiable may also represent key cost drivers, as within the standard time/cost/quality triangle (Figure 3.1), and, although it may be possible to compromise on one or two simultaneously, it will not be possible to compromise on all three. Thus, if the sponsor is not prepared to move on the time constraints for a project, there must be some scope to move on either the quality or the cost aspects of the project. This model is also applicable to the selection of suppliers, as different suppliers may offer a particular focus to their delivery which may be aligned to the requirements of the sponsor if the drivers have been pre-determined.

Responsibilities

We have already noted that a top-level scope of services should be provided as part of the

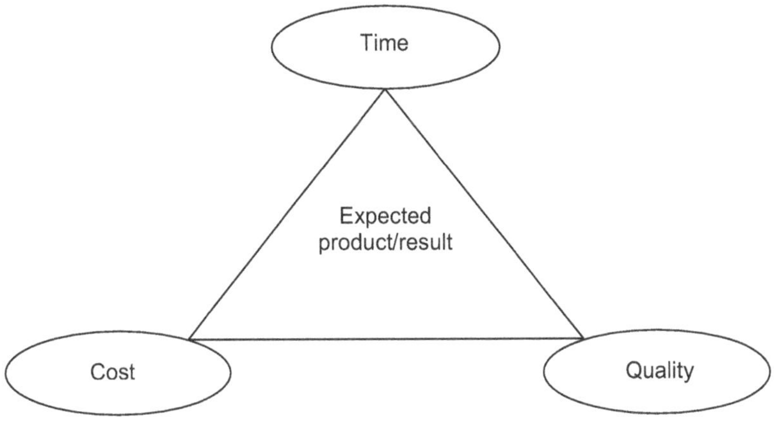

Figure 3.1 Time/cost/quality triangle

RFP package. However, this will not be detailed enough for the supplier to generate an accurate proposal. Within the scope of services, there will most often be some areas of work and activities that are to be outsourced, and some tasks that are to be performed by the sponsor. Within many sponsor companies, it is very rare for all activities to be outsourced, even for a fully outsourced project. However, this may not be the case for biotechnology companies. The International Conference on Harmonisation Guidelines on Good Clinical Practice (ICH-GCP)[1] states that 'responsibility for the quality and integrity of the trial data always resides with the sponsor' and that it is the responsibility of the sponsor to determine what level of ownership and oversight is retained when outsourcing.

Section 5.2.2 of the ICH-GCP guidelines also requires that 'any trial-related duty and function that is transferred to and assumed by a CRO should be specified in writing'. So some greater level of detail of the services to be outsourced and which party will be responsible for what activities is required, particularly if the service to be outsourced relates to clinical trial activities.

Although these requirements need not form part of the contract, it is often considered that the contract is a suitable vehicle through which the transfer and acceptance of key responsibilities can be documented as both parties will ultimately sign the contract. Even if the contract is used in this way, the detailed responsibility transfer information need not form part of the RFP. However, when combined, the RFP and the proposal will form the basis for the operational scope of the contract; it saves time (and additional documentation) and enables a comprehensive proposal to be generated if the responsibilities that are to be transferred are clarified at this early stage.

This level of detail is often contained in what is known as a task ownership matrix (TOM). Table 3.1 provides a comprehensive, although not exhaustive, example of a checklist of responsibilities for all the activities that may usefully be grouped under the heading study design while Table 3.2 summarises activities that may be considered for subsequent aspects of the proposal.

1. International Conference on Harmonisation of Technical Requirements for Registration of Pharmaceuticals for Human Use. ICH Harmonised Tripartite Guideline, Guideline for Good Clinical Practice, E6, May 1996.

Table 3.1 Task ownership matrix – study design

Activity		Detail	Budgeted hours/ days	Unit cost/hour or day	Total cost	CRO task	Sponsor task	N/A or third party
Study design								
1.	Protocol design							
2.	Protocol review							
3.	Protocol amendments							
4.	Protocol translations							
5.	CRF design							
6.	CRF review							
7.	CRF printing*							
8.	CRF translations							
9.	Informed consent – design							
10.	Informed consent – printing*							
11.	Informed consent translations							
12.	Diary cards – design							
13.	Diary cards – printing*							

*Pass-through costs anticipated

The TOM can be tailored for each piece of work to be outsourced, or alternatively can be used as a master checklist for all projects. The latter can help in ensuring that no items are overlooked and allow some degree of consistency to be built into the RFP process. Using a master checklist can also reduce rework for multiple projects, and can provide a mechanism for capturing learnings from previous outsourcing events with a view to continuously improving the RFP process.

Costs

The information in the RFP and the proposal will form the basis for negotiation (see Chapter 5) and eventually for the contract (see Chapter 7). If the contract needs to be invoiced in a certain way (for example, direct costs separate from pass-through costs) then it makes sense to request this breakout in the initial proposal. It is often useful to provide a 'budget grid' to suppliers to complete with cost information. Each supplier has its own costing structure and mechanism, and it can be very difficult to compare between them (even if the assumptions are the same) without a standard format. However, there may be some benefits to allowing suppliers to use their own costing mechanisms, particularly if consistency is not an issue and if cost is not a major consideration in the selection process. Requiring the suppliers to force fit to an artificial cost structure may delay the proposal generation process and result in errors.

The breakdown of the costs that are required should be clearly stated. Separate costs for each individual item on the checklist may be requested, as indicated on the example given. However, if this level of detail is too onerous, tasks can be grouped together and a

Table 3.2 Activities for inclusion in the task ownership matrix

Study set-up • Regulatory approvals • Import approvals • Site identification • Site assessment/ selection • Ethics approval • Ethics committee fees*	• Investigator agreements • Investigator meetings* • Monitoring manual • Training of monitors • Training of investigators • Laboratory identification and contract	• Site initiation visits • Authority to access patient data • Investigator indemnity • Study master file • Investigator files • Travel*
Drug supplier • Randomisation list • Code-breaks • Design of packaging • Drug packaging	• Design of labels • Translation of labels • Drug labelling • Instruction leaflets	• Instruction leaflets • Translation of instruction leaflets • Printing instruction leaflets
Drug management • Storage • Distribution	• Pharmacy briefing • Pharmacy payments • Accountability	• Collection from investigators • Destruction
Study management • Routine monitoring** • AE notification to sponsor • Medical review of SAEs • SAE notification to sponsor • SAE notification to authorities	• Notification of fees owing to investigator • Actioning investigator fees • Query resolution • Close-out visits	• Admin of lab supplies • Real-time access to study results • Real-time access to study management database • Travel*
Project management • Status reports** • Meetings with sponsor**	• Newsletters • AE assessment	• CRA in-house support** • Travel*
Data management • Database design/build • CRF tracking • Secondary review • Data coding	• Database documentation • Database testing • Data entry • Data monitoring administration**	• Data query generation and resolution • Exception summaries • Post finalisation changes
Statistics • Interim statistical analysis • Interim statistical report	• Final analysis • Final statistical report	• Data review • CRF tabulations • SAS datasets
Quality assurance • Site audits • Systems audits	• Database audit • Statistical report audit	• Clinical report audit • In-house audit • Travel*
Clinical study report • Write clinical report	• Publication	
Regulatory affairs • Notification of protocol amendments	• Annual safety reports to authorities**	• Expert report**

*Pass-through costs anticipated
**Must be defined

cost requested against each group of tasks. Pass-through costs should be clearly identified in the proposal (for example, travel expenses), particularly if they are to be invoiced separately from labour costs.

A spreadsheet version of the checklist may be provided to the supplier on disk, for completion and calculation of costs, and this may be combined with the checklist of responsibilities or may be supplied as a stand-alone document for completion.

'Miscellaneous' costs are a fact of life, but should be avoided if at all possible. If a supplier includes any miscellaneous costs, then they should be asked to define what these costs cover.

THE PROPOSAL

Prescriptive or creative

The way in which the RFP process is designed varies, from company to company, from service type to service type and often, in larger sponsor companies, from team to team. The basic concept of the RFP, though, is either to prescribe the format and detail which is required in the resulting proposal, or to allow the supplier to be more creative and to submit their proposal in the format and level of detail that they choose. Both approaches offer some benefits but can result in problems, and while the decision can be driven by company size, project size or other arbitrary factors, it is important to assess the aims of the RFP process and to consider the best way of achieving those aims. For example, if considering patient recruitment services, it may be of value to allow the suppliers to submit a creative proposal with story-boards and mock-ups. As long as there are sufficient points at which a reasonable and objective assessment of the proposals can be made then this may be better than trying to force a wordy textual explanation.

The aim for the sponsor is to provide consistent, comprehensive information to suppliers to enable an accurate and realistic proposal to be generated. It is not always possible to share all the relevant information with the suppliers at the RFP stage, often because it is not available. For example, it may not be clear how many sites per country are required to be monitored by the supplier. Therefore, in some cases, the RFP and subsequently the proposal will develop over time. As we have discussed, an assessment then needs to be made as to whether a prescriptive assumption is to be made by the sponsor, or if a creative proposal from the supplier will address the need.

Proposal components

The required format and content of the proposal should be explained within the RFP. In addition to the cost breakdown required, other areas may be of importance depending on the scope of outsourced services. In general a proposal will contain the following:

- services to be supplied

- how the services will be supplied
- supplier competencies and experience
- project team
- approach to project management
- risks and issues identified
- feasibility
- costs.

Feasibility is an often-underestimated part of the RFP process that can be very important in the supplier selection process. For example, when outsourcing patient recruitment services, the supplier might be asked to comment on the proposed study design, and to make an assessment of likely recruitment rates in various countries. This can be used to either confirm or challenge the expectations of the sponsor. As the assumptions are discussed and agreed between supplier and sponsor for the basis of the contract, it is important that both parties are comfortable with what is expected and what can be achieved. The proposal provides an opportunity for the supplier to raise any questions or concerns over the proposed project framework and the sponsor requirements, and a detailed and useful assessment of feasibility can offer a point of differentiation between proposals and therefore between suppliers.

If the outsourced services require experienced staff, either therapeutically or functionally, then the supplier should be asked to provide an indication of the experience of the staff that are available, and if possible those that have been identified as suitable and are proposed to work on the project. Indeed, for key staff roles such as project managers or medical writers, an appropriate curriculum vitae and/or a proposal for named staff members may be requested. Where no or only key members of staff are identified by name then it would be appropriate to consider the general turnover of operational staff within the company as this can give an indication of how stable the project team is likely to be throughout the lifetime of the project.

Where the individuals to be assigned are considered of less importance than the experience of the company in general, then a summary of previous relevant experience within an appropriate timeframe (for example, 12 months to two years) may be acceptable. In addition it might be appropriate to detail the number of previous studies of a similar size that have been successfully completed. This may be supplemented with appropriate references from other sponsors if these are available.

The proposal represents the opportunity for the supplier to tender for the work to be outsourced, and as such it represents a 'sales pitch'. How relevant, concise and clear that pitch is depends to a great extent on how comprehensive the RFP is, and in how much the requirements for the proposal are detailed.

SUPPLIER SELECTION

Once the proposals have been received by the sponsor, the selection decision can be made and the contract can then be negotiated (see Chapter 5). The mechanism for supplier selection will again depend on the scope of the work being outsourced and the quality of the proposals that are received.

When outsourcing large projects, there can be value in holding an internal review session to make an initial assessment of the proposals. At this stage if there is clear differentiation between suppliers and/or the services to be outsourced are simple, it may be possible to make a selection decision based on the proposal material alone. If, however, there are specific concerns or questions regarding some of the information, if the individuals who will be delivering the services are of particular importance, if there is no clear benefit to choosing one supplier over another, or if a creative proposal format has been delivered that requires further explanation, then it may be considered worthwhile to hold a face-to-face or 'bid defence' meeting. This meeting is often facilitated by the contract management group in larger companies, or by the project team.

Prior to scheduling a bid defence meeting, it is important to consider the focus of the meeting and the information sharing and discussion opportunities that such a meeting might afford. The more information and direction that can be shared with the suppliers in advance of the meeting, the more useful and focused the meeting is likely to be. To this end it is useful to draft an agenda which can be used to keep the meeting to time, and to ensure that the salient points are covered without the discussion being side-tracked. When outsourcing large projects, the use of functional line breakout sessions might be considered useful in order to maximise the use of the time available.

The purpose of the meeting should be to clarify areas of concern, address any specific questions, and investigate unclear proposals for delivery and/or to meet the key members of the proposed project team. Any bid defence meeting that lasts longer than half a day or so may be considered to lack focus and to be used to compensate for inadequate proposals.

It may be considered necessary to meet face-to-face with all of the potential suppliers who have submitted a proposal, or it may be possible to reduce the number of meetings by eliminating one or more suppliers on the basis of their proposals. In any case, it is important to provide a reasonable amount of notice to the suppliers regarding expectations around this meeting including required attendance, likely agenda items and focus for discussion and potential meeting dates. If the bid defence meeting strategy is considered at a sufficiently early stage, this information may be discussed and communicated at the RFP stage, helping to speed up the selection process post-proposal.

Once the proposals have been reviewed in detail by the sponsor, any clarifications have been made by the supplier and any face-to-face meetings deemed necessary have been held, it is useful for the outsourcing team to hold a de-brief session to consider all the information that has been collected during the RFP process. If the assessment can be made using pre-defined objective criteria then it may be easier to reach a consensus decision regarding the selection, particularly when outsourcing large projects involving a number of functional lines.

Once a decision has been made, the RFP process can be considered complete. All that is left to do is to negotiate the contract (see Chapter 7) and to inform the unsuccessful suppliers of the decision not to proceed with their services. For larger outsourced studies, this is often not done until successful placement of the work has been documented by the execution of a contract. In this way, the sponsor leaves their contracting options open until final resolution and placement of the work.

CONCLUSIONS

There is unlikely to be any standard RFP process or package that will address all the outsourcing needs for a particular sponsor. With the RFP, one size certainly does not fit all. However, if the RFP package is clear, comprehensive and concise, the resulting proposals are more likely to be comparable and unambiguous, making the selection of an appropriate supplier and the later generation of a contract simpler. In this way, the potential burden for both the sponsor and supplier with regard to work, re-work, resource and documentation generation and management can be optimised and managed.

Above all, it is important to take the time to think in advance about the aim of the outsourcing event, and to clarify the expectations of what will be achieved and by when. The approach, the information and the players may vary, but the basic concept remains the same, and once understood, the process and the tools can be refined to address each need as it arises.

CHAPTER 4

Risk Management

Nermeen Varawalla, *PRA International, UK*

Outsourcing in the pharmaceutical industry continues to grow in volume, variety and complexity. Outsourcing arrangements range from the complete outsourcing of a pharmaceutical company's clinical development requirements to 'insourcing' specific resources on a tactical basis. The drivers for the increase in volume and nature of clinical development outsourcing are primarily twofold. First, there is a wider variety of sponsors with growing product pipelines, that increasingly include biotechnology, small and/or virtual pharmaceutical companies. Secondly, there is a quest for increased efficiencies within the clinical trials process and a realisation that outsourcing may be able to deliver this. In order to meet the growing and varied demand for outsourced clinical development services, more and more CRO service providers continue to appear in the market place.

The ambiguity inherent in the drug development process makes it fraught with scientific and commercial risks. In addition, clinical trial outsourcing, just like any other form of outsourcing, has certain inherent risks. The key to capturing the high return that outsourcing has the potential to deliver is by identifying, understanding and managing the inherent risks.

There are risks for both parties in the outsourcing relationship, namely the pharmaceutical sponsor and the CRO. For a working relationship to be successful it is important for both groups to be cognisant of each other's risk exposure. This chapter will examine the key risks to which both parties are exposed and discuss ways to manage them effectively.

CAUSES OF RISK

There are inherent commercial risks associated with the outsourcing of clinical development which arise from the content, processes and people involved in the activity. Biomedical research, experimentation and innovation are by definition associated with the risk of failure or an unexpected outcome. However, because of the significant financial investment that drug development requires, the commercial stakes are elevated.

Every outsourcing relationship is exposed to the risks associated with transferring activities and capabilities to an external organisation with subsequent loss of internal controls. Managing the transfer of outsourced activities and the process of aligning these activities with corporate objectives is important to maximise the benefits and minimise the risks of outsourcing.

The costs and timelines for clinical development can be impacted by a number of external factors that neither party has control of. These include the following:

- the regulatory environment – decisions made by regulatory authorities can adversely impact the study timelines, budgets and even the eventual study outcome
- competitor trials and/or product launches may have a detrimental effect on patient enrolment rates and product commercialisation plans
- changes in project finances resulting from altering commitment of capital markets, venture capital and private investors can also place the study at risk.

Additionally there is intense competition within the clinical development sector. Sponsors are vying for a share of the market for their product under development. Similarly, CROs are in competition with each other to increase their respective shares of the outsourced clinical development market, and competitive pressures on both parties make them more vulnerable to increase the risk profile of their contractual agreements.

NATURE OF RISK

There is a fundamental difference in the business model of sponsors and CROs. The sponsor has a product business with financial investments and profit margins that are on a different scale from the service business model of the CRO. They have high value intellectual property, are comparatively well capitalised and enjoy relatively large profit margins. Thus, pharmaceutical sponsors have the financial depth to accommodate greater levels of risk. In contrast, CROs operate in a relatively cash-constrained environment with comparatively modest profit margins and thus have a lower appetite for risk.

Hence not surprisingly, sponsors and CROs have substantially different perspectives and attitudes to risk. Recognising these differences will contribute to effective risk management of the outsourcing relationship.

Risk for sponsors

The gravest risk for the sponsor is failure of the CRO to deliver clinical data of acceptable quality. The consequences of this could be delays in obtaining marketing authorisation for the product with loss of sales and compromised market positioning with respect to competitor products. For a biotechnology company, poor quality data could result in failure to secure a licensing agreement with major pharmaceutical companies who have relatively stringent data quality criteria. In the worst case scenario, poor data quality could require the sponsor to repeat part or whole of the study with additional expense and further loss of time.

More common but less grave is the risk of study delays with study milestones missed and the CRO unable to provide key deliverables in accordance with the contractually agreed timelines. Such delays ultimately result in financial losses for the sponsor due to delayed realisation of product sales. Moreover, individual project and contracts managers within the sponsor organisation face embarrassment and in the worst case scenario compromised career prospects.

Midway through the project, the CRO may request a change to the agreed budget resulting in one or more change orders. Increases to the study budget are a common cause of acrimony in the sponsor–CRO relationship, particularly if the sponsor is unable to accept the basis for the proposed budget extension.

The sponsor entrusts the CRO with their most precious asset, namely the intellectual property encompassed within the product under development. If this is jeopardised through carelessness by the CRO, the sponsor is exposed to major financial risk. The likelihood of such a risk is very rare; however, the impact could be substantial.

Essentially there are no differences in the risks that a biotechnology sponsor is exposed to as compared to a large pharmaceutical sponsor. However, the impact of the above risks on a smaller biotechnology company with relatively lower financial stability would be much more detrimental.

Risks for CRO

Study cancellation can be detrimental to a CRO's financial standing. On securing new business, CROs add the business to their backlog and make operational and resourcing arrangements to execute this business, often with substantial financial outlays. As detailed in Table 4.1, a number of very obvious, but nonetheless unpredictable, events could

Table 4.1 Risks faced by CROs

Unpredictable risks likely to negatively affect CRO backlog through study cancellation
• Unexpected product safety issues identified in earlier or ongoing studies
• Unexpected product efficacy issues identified in earlier or ongoing studies
• Launch of competitor products that diminish the commercial potential of the study drug
• Changes to the regulatory environment

represent a potential financial loss for the CRO. Working with biotechnology and/or small pharmaceutical companies, there is an additional risk that the sponsor company may be financially compromised following the impact of one of the above adverse factors.

Although to a lesser degree, delayed or non-payment of service fees and/or pass-through expenses will also compromise a CRO's finances, particularly if substantial investments have been made by the CRO to fund study-related expenses. Unexpected events could require additional study expenditure and, if the sponsor is unwilling to pay for this, the CRO may be forced to make these payments so as to achieve the subsequent payment milestone. Sound financial control is important for the sustainable management of a CRO's business and clearly the risk of being out of pocket during a project is of concern.

Conduct of the clinical trial carries a significant amount of trial- and/or product-related risk. Although rare, both the sponsor and CRO could be liable for the damages caused by the trial and these could be substantial.

MANAGEMENT OF RISK

Identifying and managing the risks described above is the responsibility of a number of individuals within both the sponsor and CRO. Within the sponsor company, it is usually the outsourcing or contracts manager who is accountable for risk management on the sponsor's side. Alternatively, in some companies, it may be the project manager who is charged with identifying and managing all outsourcing and project risks. Within the CRO, it is usually the contracts and legal departments that are central to risk management. In addition, the clinical project teams, finance departments and senior management of both organisations play a role in the identification and management of risk.

Including a formal risk management process as part of the outsourcing and project management process is the key to reducing risks. Indeed the identification of potential outsourcing risks should start at the same time as the development of the project scope.

Arguably, outsourcing could be a sound strategy for minimising the risks of clinical development, particularly as heavy investment in fixed overheads, such as resources, are avoided. It is not unusual for a biotechnology or small pharmaceutical company to decide that clinical operations are not a core competency they wish to develop and thus they form a strategic outsourcing relationship with one or more CROs entrusted to deliver the required clinical data.

The three main approaches to managing the risk inherent in the sponsor–CRO relationship are:

- partner selection
- contract design
- project management
- relationship management.

Partner selection

As in any commercial transaction it is usual for the buyer to enjoy the upper hand with respect to vendor selection. The sponsor does have the choice of CRO vendor and hence the opportunity to use CRO selection as a way to minimise outsourcing risks. Although the competitive dynamics of the market place give the CRO less leeway with respect to sponsor selection, a degree of caution could be valuable. Thus the approach to partner selection from both perspectives is discussed below.

CRO selection

There are a number of outsourcing models that are being deployed in the industry:

- full service outsourcing of specific clinical trials;
- 'insourcing' where named resources are hired from the CRO for specified time periods;
- functional outsourcing where the sponsor elects to outsource certain functions for one or more projects instead of the full service model;
- a hybrid model where the sponsor's clinical operations group competes with CROs for the sponsor's clinical development requirements.

Selection of the appropriate outsourcing model to meet particular requirements can be a sound approach to manage the risks of outsourcing clinical development. Effort taken to carefully select the CRO services does mitigate the risk of an unsuccessful relationship. Hence it is worthwhile for sponsors to develop and adopt a defined process for their CRO selection.

To start with, it is important to define the selection criteria which should include:

- operational capabilities
- the existence of a supporting corporate and management structure
- financial stability
- robustness of operational processes
- organisational fit.

The CRO's operational capabilities can be assessed by determining whether they have the necessary:

- experience and expertise within the relevant therapeutic areas and trial phases
- functional domains
- geographic reach to meet the sponsor's requirements.

It is also important to determine whether the CRO's operational staff adhere to processes and are well supported by systems that will deliver quality. The CRO's performance metrics may be a useful indicator of both past performance and the CRO's ability to ensure continual high performance. Assessing how the CRO controls its third party vendors and suppliers may also be important.

It is also valuable to verify the CRO's financial stability to mitigate the risk of the CRO's insolvency or acquisition during the lifetime of the project. The financial statements of publicly traded CROs are in the public domain; however, it should also be possible to assess the financial health of privately owned CROs by a series of well-chosen questions related to revenue and profitability.

More subjective measures such as the strategic and cultural fit between the CRO and the sponsor organisations are also valuable indicators of a low risk relationship. It is important to ensure that this good fit extends beyond the sponsor's contracts group to the clinical project teams. A good inter-personal relationship between staff at both organisations does contribute to a lower likelihood of friction, and its maintenance is particularly important during the most stressful parts of the project. Flexibility on the part of the CRO and engaged senior management within the CRO also bode well for a good working relationship.

The degree to which each of the above criteria should be considered and the importance placed on each will depend on the type of sponsor and the specific requirements of the project. For example, a biotechnology sponsor may be more dependent on the CRO's medical and scientific expertise whereas a large pharmaceutical sponsor would almost certainly look to its own personnel in these areas. Recognising the relative importance of these criteria in each instance will assist with wise CRO selection and, in doing so, will contribute to risk management. However, it may be that not all of the criteria considered important by the sponsor can be met by any single CRO. Thus, for example, in order to access certain geographies or specialist services, the sponsor may need to compromise on other selection criteria. Thus, a niche CRO may not be able to demonstrate long-term financial stability to the same extent as global players, but may be best placed to provide the type of contract services required. Such a compromise need not be a deterrent to engage the services of a niche CRO provided that the risks are recognised and additional safeguards put in place to mitigate them.

A number of different methods can be used to evaluate potential CROs against the selection criteria described above. These include:

- market research
- a formal Request for Information (RFI)
- the Request for Proposal (RFP) process
- visits to the CRO offices and client references
- audits of the CRO offices and personnel.

As has been discussed in detail in Chapter 2, a well-designed RFI questionnaire is a valuable tool for CRO selection and can help the sponsor to select a handful of providers that meet its key selection criteria. Taking up client references can be worthwhile when trying to ascertain the CRO's performance and track record and, if the sponsor has had the opportunity to work previously with the CRO, feedback from the project team may not only be a positive testimonial to the CRO's capabilities but can also help identify areas for future improvements.

Service costs, volume discounts and payment terms will play a part in the selection process. However, in the interest of risk management it is essential to be wary against taking on undue risk in order to achieve cost savings. For example, it is worth ensuring that a low cost data management vendor will be able to deliver the quality of data needed to meet commercial and/or regulatory requirements.

Preferred providers

Evaluating the above criteria is a time-consuming and complex exercise, so, in order to avoid repeating the selection process for every outsourcing requirement, sponsors may choose to have a group of pre-approved, preferred providers. Following thorough due diligence, sponsors select their preferred providers who are then almost exclusively considered for all the sponsor's future outsourcing requirements. The mix of preferred providers should include an appropriate range of both large, global CROs as well as niche speciality providers. Similarly, the suitability and performance of these preferred providers should be reviewed periodically, ideally, every two to three years.

Adopting the preferred provider approach for CRO selection and restricting CRO choice to a group of carefully selected preferred providers offers the sponsor a number of advantages which all contribute to better managing the risk of the relationship. Having a limited number of suppliers enables the sponsor to have a better control over each of them with opportunities for swift problem resolution, more efficient resource management and standardisation of working practices. Sponsors are more inclined to invest the time and effort to building a better working relationship with their providers. The transparency and trust that would be built in such a relationship greatly facilitates joint working. Working with preferred providers, however, does carry the risk of complacency on both sides and this should be addressed by regular reviews of existing preferred providers and the introduction of new ones.

The methods for preferred provider selection are similar to those described above, but the crucial difference is that the potential longevity of the relationship and the promise of high business volume incentivises the sponsor to be more thorough in its due diligence and the CRO to be more accommodating in the discussions of commercial terms.

Sponsor selection

Being in a competitive market place makes it difficult and unusual for CROs to turn away business. However, a certain degree of caution with respect to taking on both new clients and new projects will enable the CRO to better manage their risk. This vigilance is even more important when dealing with biotechnology and small pharmaceutical companies and CROs with the opportunity to work with such organisations should undertake the necessary due diligence to ascertain the sponsor's financial standing and their ability to fund the project.

In addition it is advisable for the CRO to assess the protocol and study requirements to ensure that they have the capabilities to successfully execute the study. It is also worth ensuring that by accepting the contract the CRO is not incurring inappropriate clinical or scientific risk. Feasibility assessment is a good way to evaluate a study protocol in particular with respect to patient and investigator enrolment. In addition, specific risks can be considered through the feasibility, such as:

- countries with limited patient population
- tests and evaluations which could be an issue
- inclusion/exclusion criteria which impact patient recruitment
- potential ethical issues regarding trial design.

In situations where the sponsor has had to change CRO mid-way through a project, it is particularly important for the new CRO to investigate precisely why their predecessor was unable to meet the sponsor's requirements as these factors are likely to be a significant risk for the incumbent CRO.

Contract design

The binding contractual agreement between the sponsor and CRO is an important formal tool to manage the risk inherent within this relationship. In order to provide the necessary safeguards for both the sponsor and the CRO, certain key areas must be covered by a legally binding contract. These include protection of the sponsor's intellectual property, mutual confidentiality and liability.

In order to safeguard the sponsor's key asset, namely their intellectual property, it is important for the contract to specify that the sponsor remains the sole, rightful owner of all the intellectual property generated through the course of the project. Both parties need to agree to abide by a two-way confidentiality agreement and commit to not disclosing any confidential information that they gain access to as a consequence of their working relationship. Stipulation of a penalty should there be a breach of confidentiality may also be included.

Liability

In recognition of the uncertainties of clinical development, the CRO cannot be expected to provide a warranty that the planned clinical trial will meet its scientific objective, be it proof of concept or regulatory approval. However, in order to cover the potential losses incurred by the sponsor as a direct consequence of mistakes made by the CRO, sponsors will seek to include a liability clause in the contract. The financial consequences for a sponsor of poor data quality or a delay in generating clinical data could be far reaching. Arguably they could cost the sponsor many millions of US dollars in lost product sales or the loss of a licensing opportunity. Understandably though, CROs are usually unwilling to bear liability for these losses and seek to restrict their liability to the costs of repeating the unsatisfactory work.

An issue of contention could be whether there is an agreed cap on this liability. In order to manage their own financial risks and limit insurance premiums, CROs are keen to avoid contracts with uncapped liability. It is usual for CROs to seek to cap their liability to two to four times the value of the service contract. The alternative would be to fix the cap at a defined cash amount which is deemed adequate to cover the costs of repeating the trial. A dispute could arise when a particular provider is contracted to provide only select services but expected to bear liability for all clinical trial services that may be required to be repeated as a consequence of their errors. In such instances both parties would need to compromise and agree on a cap that is commensurate with the value of the CRO's contracted services rather than to the estimated costs of repeating the entire study. The CRO is expected to demonstrate insurance cover that would be adequate to cover the liability payments should the need arise.

A very serious, though rare, risk for the CRO is liability from damage caused by the study drug or the trial itself. In order to manage this risk, the CRO should ensure that the sponsor is contractually bound to indemnify the CRO and its sub-contractors, including investigators, from all third party claims arising from the study. For added security the sponsor should indemnify for unlimited costs of settlement and reasonable legal costs.

Definition of costs

Keeping in mind the uncertainties of clinical development and the consequent likelihood of changes to the proposed project plan, it is worth making an effort at the outset to manage the risks of changes in the project scope and budget. This is best done by clear documentation of the responsibilities and expected deliverables of the various participants, including the sponsor and its local operating companies, the CRO and any additional third party vendors. This may be supplemented by an 'activity plan' that details the scope of the project and the specific services to be provided along with the timelines and milestones for key deliverables. A communication plan that describes the arrangements for the flow of information between the two organisations could be an important addendum.

In principle, the clearer the scope provided to the CRO, the more accurate the CRO will be when providing costings. It is worth considering holding a meeting or teleconference with the bidding CROs to provide a thorough briefing, particularly if the project is complicated. This way, all CROs get the same information and have a chance to clarify any details before the proposal is completed.

It is also important that the sponsor's contracts or project manager provides details of any changes in scope to the CROs in a timely fashion in order that any revisions to the project budget can be made.

The project budget with services fees and pass-through costs, which may include investigator grants, is an important part of the contractual agreement. Other financial issues that require to be clarified are the payment schedule and payment terms. In the interest of the project it is important to ensure that the CRO remains in a cash-neutral position for the duration of the study so that there is always cash available to fund the study requirements. Practically this is achieved by a payment schedule that is structured so as to include an up-front payment prior to the commencement of any work that is deemed to be adequate to fund study start up, usually 15–20 per cent of the total budget. There may be room for negotiation in deciding the extent of the up-front payment which is determined by the total estimate for CRO services, duration of the project and the financial stability of the sponsor. The remainder of the payments could be structured as regular installments or linked to key study milestones. The last payment is usually valued at less than 10 per cent of the total budget and linked to one of the final study deliverables. For the CRO to manage project-related cash flows, payment terms that offer a 30–45 day period for the payment of invoices are usually specified.

The contract should also describe the procedure for managing the study pass-through expenses. Pass-through expenses are mainly related to investigator fees, vendor fees and travel expenses. The risk of the CRO being out of pocket due to extension of the pass-through budget is mitigated by separating these costs from the CRO service fees, although the CRO will often handle these payments on behalf of the sponsor.

Given the global nature of the pharmaceutical industry, project costs can be affected by exchange rate fluctuations, which can represent a significant risk to both parties. It is therefore advisable for both parties to agree on the exchange rates that will be used for the length of the study as well as the measures they will adopt if there are unexpected exchange rate fluctuations. To avoid disagreements it is useful to agree on the extent of exchange rate fluctuation that would merit a budget revision and also on the source for exchange rate information.

Changes of the proposed CRO staff either before project kick-off or midway through the project can be a cause of much frustration for the sponsor. At an individual level, personal and professional developments make staff changes inevitable. Hence, it is important to establish an agreed process for managing these changes with, if necessary, the inclusion of a penalty clause in the event of non-compliance by the CRO.

As change orders are a common risk for outsourced projects it is worth agreeing on the basis and process for handling changes in scope of the project. Up-front detailed clarification of the activities and costs will facilitate managing the subsequent scope changes. Good communication and thorough documentation of the project scope changes will also assist with the management of the change order process.

There are a number of reasons why part-way through a project, the sponsor may decide to terminate it. These include product safety and/or efficacy issues and occasionally unsatisfactory CRO performance. In order to safeguard the CRO from losses following study termination, it is helpful to establish a clear procedure for project termination. If the cause of termination is unrelated to CRO performance the sponsor would usually be required to provide the CRO with a 90-day notice period. During this time the CRO can institute a 'wind-down' plan so as to safely complete the project close-out activities. The sponsor is expected to cover the costs incurred by the CRO as a result of premature project termination including those of the wind-down plan.

It is rare for the relationship between the sponsor and CRO to break down to the extent that either party feels the need to resort to legal action. However, as this unwelcome outcome does remain a possibility, it is worth setting out the position with respect to important legal issues such as the role for arbitration and which country's jurisdiction governs the contract. Arrangements need to be in place for both internal quality assurance and external groups, for example regulatory authorities, to gain access to a copy of the contract between the sponsor and CRO.

Master Services Agreement

Entering into a Master Services Agreement (MSA) with a CRO can save the sponsor time and money. Equally importantly it can also put them in a strong position with respect to the management of inherent risk, particularly in the areas of liability, insurance, confidentiality, protection of the sponsor's intellectual property rights and any agreed commercial terms such as payment schedules or discounted rates. MSAs are covered in more detail in Chapter 6.

Contract types

There are a number of ways to structure the service agreements and contracts so as to safeguard the sponsor from the risk of the CRO being unable to meet the quality, timeline and budgetary expectations. These are described in detail in Chapter 6 and summarised here.

Fixed-price contracts

Prior to project start the CRO makes a binding commitment to deliver the project within the fixed budget. Hence, unless the sponsor requests a change in study scope, namely an increase in the number of patients, sites and/or case report form (CRF) pages, the CRO is unable to claim any additional service fees for the study. The advantage of such a contract for the sponsor is release from the risk of change orders and budget creep. This is of particular value for biotechnology and small pharmaceutical companies which are reliant on external funds to finance their clinical development projects and where risks of budget increase can be a significant problem.

It is also possible to structure a fixed-price contract so as to manage the risk of escalation of the study pass-through costs. The CRO would prepare the pass-through budget on the basis of a feasibility assessment and prior experience, and commit to delivering the project within this fixed budget provided there were no changes to the project scope. In such a situation the CRO would be incentivised to keep the pass-through expenses below the budget.

Unit-price contracts

In this case, the project is divided into discrete deliverables of limited size such as monitoring visits, data transfers and monthly project management, each of which has an individual price, and the CRO is paid on delivery of these discrete pieces of work. This deliverable links the payment schedule with perceived transparency of the CRO's pricing structure and facilitates the management of the risk of change orders and budget extensions.

Outcomes-based contracts

These types of contracts can represent a high risk to the CRO unless carefully evaluated at the feasibility stage of the project, and appropriately costed. Payments are linked to the delivery of previously agreed study milestones such as initiation of all sites, enrolment of all patients or database lock by certain dates. In addition it is possible to include a bonus or penalty clause should the CRO exceed or fail to meet expectations. Positive incentives tend to be more effective than penalties; however it must be remembered that for the CRO the greatest incentive to meet the sponsor's expectation is the promise of repeat business. Conversely, loss of a customer and/or reputation in a competitive market place is a severe penalty for the CRO.

Product risk sharing contracts

A handful of CROs have entered contractual arrangements where *in lieu* of a complete or partial payment of their service fees they are awarded an equity stake in the sponsor company or a percentage of the out-licensing fees or product sales. These CROs are operating within a hybrid business model with elements of both a service and product business. Curiously such a model does position the CRO as a competitor to other pharmaceutical sponsors. The CRO is exposed to the risks of product performance and will be impacted by product safety and efficacy as well as the product's commercial success. Although CROs are keen to be development partners for their customers, very few are willing to help finance the sponsor's clinical development programme and take on the potential risks and benefits of the product's commercial performance.

Project management

Skilled project management will make a substantial contribution to mitigating the project-related risks. Good project management includes a well-defined framework for project conduct that is established at the project kick-off meeting with buy-in from stakeholders both in the CRO and sponsor organisations. Figure 4.1 demonstrates the key components of a project plan. Clear definition of roles and responsibilities along with performance metrics for both the CRO and the sponsor form the foundation for this governance framework.

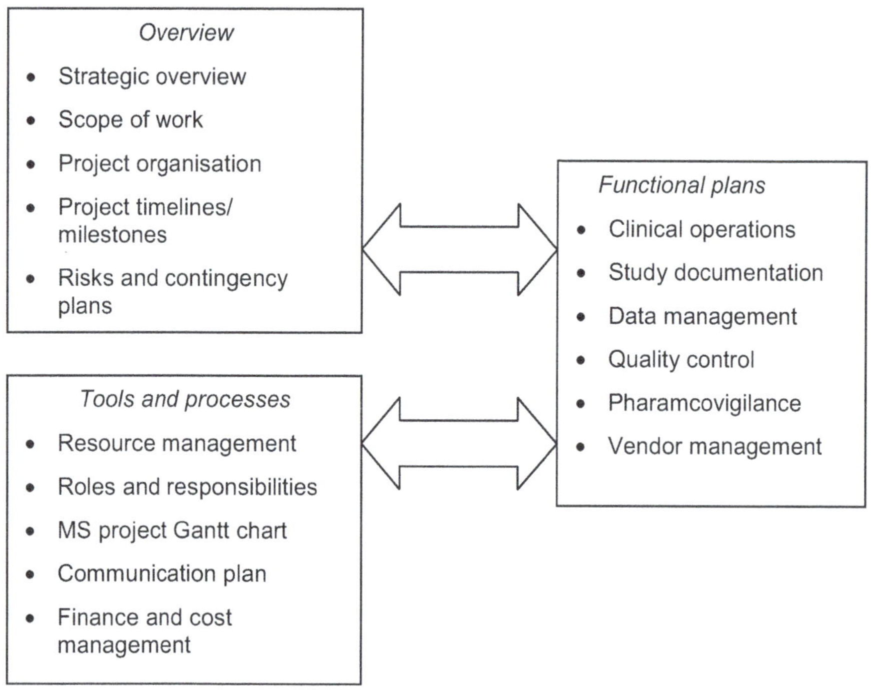

Figure 4.1 Project plan

Sound project management includes identification and listing of the project risks at the time of project start up. Examples of common project risks are listed in Table 4.2.

Table 4.2 Common project risks

Common project risks
• Delays in obtaining regulatory approvals • Delays in site initiation • Delays with patient recruitment • Difficulties with the management of clinical trial supplies • Issues with vendors • Delays with the processing of CRFs • Utilisation of resources at a level that exceeds the budget

By tracking key project metrics, as shown in Figure 4.2, it would be possible to identify project risk in a timely fashion.

Clinical operations	*Data management*	*Contractual*
• Start-up metrics	• Data entry	• Deliverables
• Enrolment metrics	• Data review	• Metrics
• CRF backlog	• Data quality	• Change order

Figure 4.2 Project status tracking: key metrics for early identification of project risk

Contingency plans should be in place for each of the main project risks which can be implemented when there is evidence that the project will be adversely affected. Contingencies could include those outlined in Figure 4.3.

Clear lines of communication, with agreement and provision for issue escalation, as well as scope for implementation of contingency arrangements, are essential for this approach to work.

In order to mitigate the risk of poor quality data, the sponsor should reserve the right, following a short notice period, to conduct inspections and audits of the CRO's standard operating procedures (SOPs), study documents and data records.

Relationship management

Effort on the part of both the sponsor and the vendor to effectively manage their working relationship throughout the project life will substantially contribute to reducing the risk of disappointments and failed expectations for both parties. Inability of the sponsor to share expectations regarding project deliverables and conduct with the CRO could result in the CRO misplacing resources and efforts to project components that represent relatively less value for the sponsor. Apart from creating inefficiencies this could lead to sponsor dissatisfaction. The CRO has the expertise to make important contributions to

Site activation/selection

Assess feasibility and activation metrics

- Redistribute sites
- Select back-up sites
- Activation incentives
- Resolve any contractual and/or Institutional Review Board/Ethics Committee issues

Patient recruitment

Monitor per site accrual and accrual metrics

- Intensify direct site support
- Protocol, study procedure or financial adjustments
- Enhance site communication
- Employ recruitment tools (for example, call centres, advertising, and so on)

Resourcing

Evaluate staff assignments, efficiency ratios and backlogs

- Apply back-up assignments
- Assign additional staff to ensure quality and speed (for example, co-monitoring)

Figure 4.3 Contingency planning

project success at both a strategic and tactical level. In the absence of a good relationship between the CRO and sponsor, these inputs may not be captured with a resulting loss for the project.

Communication is the key to any successful relationship, and poor or unclear communication represents a significant risk to the project. It is important that a formal plan for regular communication between both organisations via status reports is developed and preferably tested prior to the start of the project. This plan should consider:

- What is to be communicated and to whom?
- How is it to be communicated?
- When is it to be communicated?

The plan could include details of:

- joint steering committees

- training workshops
- project review meetings and teleconferences
- email correspondence.

However, it is important that such a formal plan should not replace opportunities for informal communication including access to senior management. A clear process for issue identification and escalation would curtail potential risk factors before the occurrence of serious consequences. It is useful for the sponsor's project team to retain contact with their contracts manager so as to be able to communicate in a timely manner any issues that may impact the contract such as protocol amendments, changes in timelines and scope of services.

The development of mutual trust and respect plays an important role in any high value outsourcing relationship and reduces the project risks. Recognition of each other's skills and capabilities will help develop this and, if CROs are treated like partners instead of suppliers, there are additional benefits to be gained particularly in terms of aligning CRO efforts with the sponsor's clinical development goals. Oversight from senior management in both organisations is valuable for relationship management and issue resolution. Particularly in a long-term CRO–sponsor relationship that extends beyond specific projects, it is worth ensuring that there are mechanisms in place to facilitate learning, share best practices and implement process improvements. A valuable opportunity to do so would be at a post-project review before the project team is disbanded whereby feedback from the various subgroups such as project managers, clinical monitors, data managers, quality assurance and finance staff could be collated.

Furthermore, for sponsors which use multiple CROs it is worth attempting to capture and implement the learnings from different interactions to all outsourcing activities. An extension of this 'lessons learnt' philosophy is for the sponsors to make an effort to 'build the ideal supplier' by encouraging the CRO to build resources and processes customised to meet the sponsor's requirements.

Aside from the sponsor–CRO relationship, it is important to pay attention to the relationships of both these parties with sites and investigators. Strong relationships at this level could contribute to improved collaboration at the site level with a mitigation of the risk of budget and timeline extension.

CONCLUSIONS

It will be many years before simulated clinical development and in-silico trials will begin to diminish the uncertainties and risks of drug development. In the meantime, it remains imperative for both the sponsor and CRO to understand each other's risks and implement ways to manage them. In achieving this, both parties will be able to truly leverage the full potential value of pharmaceutical outsourcing.

CHAPTER 5

Negotiation

Jim Cannon, *Cannon Associates*

The art of finding resolution to disputes that last[1]

It was Oscar Wilde who said that a 'cynic is a man who knows the price of everything and the value of nothing'. The same might be said of a poor negotiator. Negotiation is successful when each of the parties to the bargain has paid a price (financial or otherwise) that they consider fair, relative to the value they each place on what they have obtained.

THE CONCEPT OF VALUE

When we purchase something, we might think it is expensive at one pound or cheap at £10 000. Our perception will always depend on the value we place on the goods or services in question and their value will vary according to a number of criteria:

- *Need.* If it is a question of life and death, especially where we are emotionally involved, price becomes less relevant. So, in the context of clinical research, need resolves around the consequences for the pharmaceutical sponsor of not completing the trial on time or not recruiting the right number of patients. How valuable are they?

- *Alternatives.* Where the order of magnitude is broadly understood, for example, when buying a car, we make comparisons between models and extras and features, rather than other goods or services. Often the context of the purchase sets the price which in other contexts might seem excessive. Thus, we are prepared to pay more for a car radio or a cup of tea in an exclusive hotel. We might also compare the cost against alternative ways of satisfying the need. For example, instead of driving to work we

1. The material in this chapter is based on the course workbook for 'Advanced Negotiation' developed for the PCMG by the Chartered Institute of Personnel and Development.

might take the train. We might also consider the opportunity cost, that is, what else could we do with the money we have put aside for the purchase? Would we rather buy a new car or go on holiday? Alternatives for a pharma might be different suppliers, countries or protocols.

- *The return, financial or otherwise, that I can make from the transaction.* If by buying a better car I break down less often and am therefore able to work more effectively, higher value is perceived in the more expensive car. Thus, in a clinical trial, the quality of the trial data might be considered as the return versus the cost of obtaining it.

APPROACHES TO NEGOTIATION

Having gained an understanding of how we value goods and services, how do we negotiate to obtain them at what we perceive to be the right cost? Over the years, three basic approaches to negotiation have emerged:

- *Streetwise ploys.* Here, much like the gladiatorial contest, negotiation is seen as a battle of wits and wills, and subterfuge is used to gain an advantage.

- *Principled negotiations* as exemplified by Fisher and Ury (1999) in their book *Getting to Yes*. In this approach, both parties expose the issues they face and their separate interests and move towards exploring the implications of each and the options for resolution. The aim is to find common ground and build on it to find a mutually acceptable solution.

- *Phased trading.* In this approach, negotiation is seen as a process and the objective is to work through the process in order to strike a bargain.

This chapter will explore each of these three approaches before developing a synthesis and examining some of the key behaviours which are essential for successful negotiation in practice.

Streetwise tactical ploys

Gavin Kennedy (2001) describes three ploys characterised by Chester Karass who promoted streetwise tactics to negotiation in the 1970s: The 'Bogey', the 'Krunch' and the 'Nibble'. Others have added to these and a selection of such tactics is outlined below:

The 'Bogey'

'I love the product but I have a limited budget.'

By the buyer making it clear that they like the product, but not at the proposed price, the seller is forced to look for ways of trimming unnecessary elements and, maybe, costs. Equally, when the seller does this, the buyer is forced to identify their real needs. However, having effectively resulted in a price reduction, this approach may confirm the buyer's suspicion that all prices *are* padded in order to provide room for manoeuvre and the seller's belief that all prices *should* be padded to protect them from the buyer's bogey.

The 'Krunch'

'You have got to do better than that.'

When faced with a proposition that is unacceptable, the buyer can use this option to signal clearly to the seller that their offer is unreasonable. The seller is forced to decide whether they have any room to manoeuvre and may well be glad to have the chance to make another offer. In the long run, like the Bogey, this approach can encourage padding of prices in order that the seller retains their margins even after reducing the price or agreeing to provide additional valuable services.

'The Nibble' or 'Salami'

'Shave the price, shave the product.'

Nibbling occurs when either party continues to exploit every avenue to further their position. A variation of this strategy is to agree what you can get, but then rather than close the negotiation, continue to nibble away to get more. Thus, in the context of outsourced clinical drug development, just when you think you have reached full agreement and the trial sponsor is about to sign the contract, they make a throw-away comment such as, 'Monitoring travel costs are included, aren't they?' In this scenario, the buyer is hoping that the seller will succumb to the urge to accept this concession purely to get the contract signed.

Buyers typically nibble by:

- paying late;
- taking unearned discounts; and
- requesting special services for free such as reports, training and consultancy.

But sellers have the opportunity to nibble too, typically by:

- providing more services and then charging for them;
- not providing all services agreed; and
- reducing the priority of delivering the services or goods, resulting in delay.

Exploration

Here each party make a careful exploration of their position relative to their opponent's, and looks for needs that the other party wants and values that they can supply easily or cheaply. These are then traded according to the other party's perception of value which clearly may be very different to yours.

Aim high

Those with low aspirations made the largest concessions in an experiment, but those with high aspirations made smaller concessions and failed fewer times. (Chester Karass)

The theory behind this tactic reflects the idea that the initial stage of any negotiation is to find the basic parameters within which both parties can work. Aiming high establishes a reference point and so sets expectations about likely outcomes. However, it is self-defeating to those who know the game. For example, it is well-known to locals that the norm in an Egyptian Souk is for the seller to ask for five times the price he will ultimately settle for.

Play it cool

In negotiation, playing it cool generally means keeping silent. By doing this, you force the other side to speak up, make a move or even offer a concession.

In my time and place

By keeping the other party waiting and ensuring the negotiation takes place on your territory or at least on one that is neutral, you effectively gain a psychological advantage through feeling in control of the situation.

Last-minute wavering

In this scenario, just when you thought you had a deal, last-minute doubts creep in from the other party about whether they want to go through with it. The tactic is designed to put pressure on the provider to agree to last-minute concessions on the basis that having spent a lot of time on the deal, the provider will do whatever it takes to avoid losing it. The counter is to move back to conditional trading and reply with a statement such as 'If we were to consider these new demands, we would need to look again at . . .'

The early concession

Giving something away early encourages the other party to reciprocate and, provided you have given careful thought as to what you can happily concede, can lead to a mutually successful outcome.

Surprise

The element of surprise can work well in negotiation, though it also has the capacity to backfire. The approach involves making a sudden shift in tactic such as suddenly becoming very angry after being icy calm, bringing a new and unexpected demand to the table or changing negotiators. In theory, the other party will be caught off-guard and agree to a request they might otherwise have fought against.

Fait accompli

This tactic is most often used in times of conflict and is essentially an 'invade and negotiate later' approach. In commercial contexts, it is seen when a deal is so far completed that it is difficult for another party to change anything.

Bland withdrawal

'Oh I am sorry, I didn't know...'

In this situation, one party forges on ahead relentlessly until found out, but then gives in without resistance in the hope that they have gained some ground before being found out.

Apparent withdrawal

This tactic requires one party to withdraw in the substantive negotiation giving the illusion to the other side that they have won, before then attacking by a different route. Wellington famously used to get his front to retreat while leaving his flanks in place in order that the enemy was drawn into a three-sided battle. A version of this is 'feinting' where you encourage your opponent to concentrate on one aspect of the deal while you move on a different front. Commercially, this tactic can occur when you are secretly negotiating with another party. Just when the major party thinks they have won concessions and the deal is concluded, you switch to the secret party.

Reversal

Very simply, this tactic involves doing the opposite of what might be expected, in the same way as one way to make money on the stock market is to do the reverse of everyone else.

Limits

'We will not negotiate past today.'

By creating limits, pressure is created to conclude negotiations – though clearly if someone else's limits don't suit you, you shouldn't feel bound by them. Natural time limits occur at the end of the day, end of the week, just before a holiday and so on.

We are friends

This approach encourages recognition of common interests and a move towards joint problem-solving. Note that it often helps to sit on the same side of the table to encourage the feeling that you really are on the same side.

Association

Here, you use the prestige of your position or your organisation to argue that your opponent will gain some benefit by being associated with you, and that as a result they should be more willing to make concessions. Several well-known companies use this tactic to negotiate down consulting fees on the grounds that the consultant would gain advantage by being able to cite this prestigious company as a client.

Differentiation

In this situation, you argue that because you are different from everyone else you deserve special treatment.

Blanketing

Here you inundate your opponent with evidence, facts and figures. It has a similar impact to fait accompli in that you have the capacity to counter every argument your opponent raises with a blizzard of information that demonstrates that a point or, perhaps more importantly, an objection has already been recognised and dealt with.

Randomising

Faced with what appears to be a bluff, this strategy argues that if you call the bluff on random occasions, you will end up in a stronger position than if you repeatedly tried to guess whether or not the bluff was genuine.

Lies, damn lies and statistics

Selective use of statistics – the politicians' trick. Certain statistics can be chosen to prove a particular point despite there being other statistics that might disprove the same point. Statistics can give the illusion of greater authenticity and rigour, which on careful analysis might prove unfounded.

Agent

If a negotiation is getting difficult, it is a useful tactic to claim that you must check back with those on whose behalf you are acting and call for an adjournment in order to do this, thereby gaining time to plan your next move. A variation of this tactic sees it combined with the nibble; just as you have reached the point of agreement, the other party says that they must check with the boss, only to return a few minutes later with a fresh demand.

Shifting levels

When faced with a sensitive issue or a sticking point, it can be useful to move the problem to a broader issue and try and agree on principles. A variation is where the big decision is deferred by agreeing to smaller decisions. For example, if you were buying a car, a sales rep might ask what colour you would choose if you were to buy? You answer 'Red', and the sales rep quickly responds with an early presumptive close, 'Let me see if we have one in stock ... yes we have and it could be delivered tomorrow.' It moves the discussion to easier ground, creates momentum and assumes without mentioning it that the buyer is seriously interested. Another classic sales example is when the sales person asks whether they can see you on Tuesday or Thursday, assuming that the decision to see them has already been made.

Projecting into the future

This approach shifts the conversation to hypothesising about the future. Phrases like 'Assuming we can strike a deal, what could be the benefits we might both enjoy?' starts the other party thinking about the future in a positive light.

Conditional trading

By using questions such as 'If we could solve this problem, would you be prepared to ...?' or 'if you could ... then we could ...' it is possible to keep all options in play and to make achievement of our opponent's goals conditional on our achieving one of ours. Other useful phrases include:

- 'What if we …? How would you feel about that?'
- 'How about …? Would that be of interest to you?'

Principled negotiation

While streetwise stratagems have been used for decades and it is good to know them, especially if they are being used against you, many of them invariably end up in a soured relationship characterised by remorse, resentment, recrimination and revenge. If either party feels that they have in some way been duped into a deal that is disadvantageous, they will certainly be more wary next time and an atmosphere of mistrust begins to develop.

Fisher and Ury (1999) sought to move beyond these tactics to find a more principled approach. They suggest that there are four key themes in successful negotiations that endure beyond a single transaction:

- Separate the people from the issue. The more emotionally aroused we become, the less likely we are to think logically. Brain chemistry suggests that when we become emotional, the limbic system becomes more active and the neocortex – the thinking part of the brain – becomes less dominant. Thus when we are in an emotional state, we find it difficult to think straight.

- Focus on interests rather than positions. As US Senator George Mitchell said: 'Nations and individuals ultimately act out of regard to their self interests.' Fundamental interests such as our desire to hold on to our job, our fears about losing face, and our worries about not meeting budget are the drivers of our commercial behaviour. As Fisher and Ury (1999) explain, 'Your position is something you have decided upon. Your interests are what caused you to decide.' Seeking to satisfy each other's interests is likely to be more fruitful than battering each other's positions.

- Identify and generate options – this helps to keep the negotiation fluid and both parties engaged.

- Use objective criteria to base the result. Particularly where one party has to make concessions, agreement is more likely to be reached when they can make reference to some objective criteria. An example might be where the cost per patient in a trial has previously been established. The price for future contracts becomes based on the maths, with negotiation confined to the exceptions.

Another key theme that emerges from this school of negotiation is the idea of Best Alternative To a Negotiated Agreement (BATNA). This approach encourages a negotiator to consider what would happen if they walk away from the negotiation? If your BATNA is better than what is on the table, then you can relax and keep on negotiating.

While widely used and admired as a professional approach, principled negotiations suffer from one big problem – it takes two to tango. If the other party is a street fighter, it becomes difficult to stick to the principled approach.

Phased trading

Gavin Kennedy (2001), building on the earlier work of Anne Douglas in the 1960s, set out an eight-step process which he claims all negotiations go through. He believes the advantage of this approach is that negotiators know where they are and where they are heading.

The eight phases are described simply as:

- Prepare
- Argue
- Signal
- Propose
- Package
- Bargain
- Close
- Agree.

APPROACHES TO NEGOTIATION: A SUMMARY

A summary and synthesis of all three approaches – streetwise tactics, principled negoatiation, phased trading – can be formulated into a practical process involving the following seven steps.

1. Prepare thoroughly

- What do you know about the other party, what has been your shared history?
- Have you thought about your BATNA?
- What are you prepared to trade for what?
- What do you really value? What would be a deal breaker and what would be a deal maker?
- Can you understand the other party's position before embarking on the negotiation, that is, can you see how to both counter their argument and give some comfort to their interests?

2. Open carefully to set the scene and establish rapport

Cultures vary greatly with regard to the amount of social 'small talk' that is appropriate before negotiations proper can start. I recall being advised 'Never talk about business until the third cup of coffee' before first doing business in the Middle East, but to some

Americans this would seem an excessive waste of time. So understanding culture is important, but in addition, can we position all conversations to achieve a more common understanding?

In my early career I regularly negotiated with trade unions. One day I entered the room and sat opposite the official ready, in my mind, to do battle. He picked up his chair and came and sat alongside me and said, 'Now Jim, how are we going to solve this problem?' He had changed the dynamics of both the room and the conversation. No longer was it a negotiation between us because the problem was no longer between us. The problem was out there in front of us both. We were on the same side of the table and, metaphorically, on the same side in solving the problem. It became a shared undertaking to find a solution, reinforced by simple embedding of positive language – 'how are *we* going to *solve* this problem?' Previously such conversations might have descended into name calling or provocative language – 'When are you going to sort out this mess?'

3. Explore each party's needs and interests

Can we find common ground? India and Pakistan have disputed ownership of Kashmir for more than 50 years. In the latest round of peace talks, they began by identifying what they agreed upon and found considerable common interests, not least that they both wished to improve the economic prosperity of the region. Moving to a higher level they found mutual interests and an opportunity to forge a bridge. Clearly, reducing personal fear, suspicion and animosity and creating a sense of progress by agreeing on some things, helps generate forward momentum in a negotiation. This is demonstrated very simply by the story of two people who both wanted a pumpkin. They fought over it and only achieved some resolution when they explored their needs and found that one wanted the flesh for soup and the other the skin for a Halloween lantern.

4. Be creative about options and alternatives

Develop options and creative ideas without committing. At this stage it is essential that both parties feel that not every word would be seized on and held to. Conditional trading (for example, 'If we could solve this problem, would you be prepared to ...?') and projecting into the future (for example, 'Assuming we can deal with this issue, what are the benefits we would both enjoy by this contract ...?') are useful tactics here.

Questions such as 'What would have to happen for this not to be a difference between us?' or 'What would you need to have happen for you to be flexible around this point?' are both approaches towards exploring different 'as if' scenarios.

5. Use objective criteria to evaluate options and best course of action

Ultimately, any agreement will only stick if it is seen as fair and reasonable to each side. A test of reasonableness is what a court might decide (remember the Unfair Contracts Terms Act). Other criteria might be the cost comparison with industry benchmarks, previous contracts, the judgements of respected experts, or the logical consequences for each side of the proposed bargain. In one negotiation, one side reacted to the other's unreasonable demand by describing in detail, and without exaggeration, how it was impossible to fulfil the conditions and suggesting that they build up between them a quotation based on a true analysis of the actual costs of fulfilling the conditions. This approach, sometimes called 'open book', moved the conversation to one based on more factual matters of what should be included in the programme of work.

6. Clarify agreement at the close to ensure that there are no loose ends or misunderstandings

In one case, an agreement to submit reports bi-weekly was interpreted by one side to mean every two weeks, while the other side thought it meant twice a week. Even where English is the first language of both parties, it is easy to see how misunderstandings can arise.

7. Review relationship and outcomes

If, on reflection, there is resentment on either side, the chances of negotiations being reopened are reduced or of either side taking action to recover what they believe to be a fair position are greatly increased. Typical actions on the side of the supplier might be cutting corners or reducing quality if they feel they have been too tightly held on price, while 'nibbling' at extra demands might be the behaviour of a purchaser who feels they have paid too much.

Always remember that it is never too late to relax your requirements if you feel that such a change might result in significant upsides in the relationship. In the pharma industry, where relationships carry on from project to project and many people have worked with each other in different roles and organisations, it is worth viewing the negotiation in the context of a longer-term relationship rather than a single transaction.

BEHAVIOURAL SKILLS IN NEGOTIATION

However much we may want to codify negotiation into a set of processes and rules, it is important to remember that it is also a relationship between people, subject to all the idiosyncrasies that people exhibit. Thus, our ability to influence behaviour needs to be effective if any of the foregoing processes are to succeed.

When two people start a conversation, the process looks something like that shown in Figure 5.1. The person on the left has a feeling and/or a thought which they wish to communicate and which is subconsciously encoded into an appropriate form depending on factors such as the individual's position, personality and culture. A medium for the communication is selected and as much may be communicated by a shrug of the shoulders or a look in the eye as in spoken words. The person on the right will hear and see this communication and decode it. If this is the first time of meeting, a shrug of the shoulders might easily be misinterpreted. The receiver on the right integrates the information into what is already in their brain. How novel is this behaviour, does it lead them to certain expectations and conclusions, some or all of which might be false?

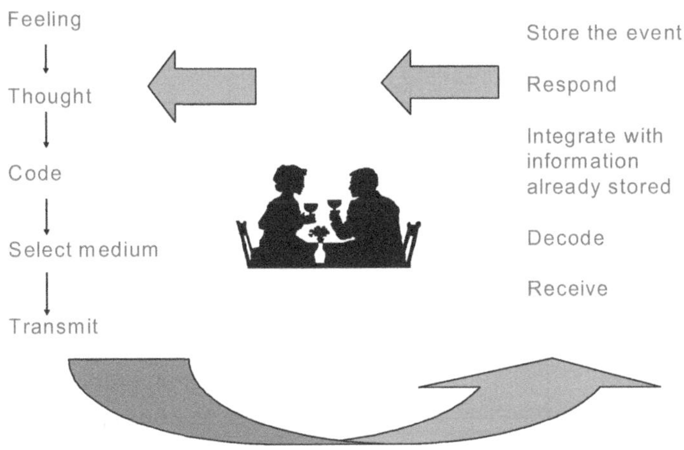

Figure 5.1 The communication process

I once heard two people at a conference talking about SMEs. It was some time before it became clear that one of them was talking about 'small and medium enterprises' while the other thought he was discussing 'system maintenance engineers'. The risk of this type of misunderstanding or miscommunication is greatly increased when language translation is also involved. The story is told of Kurt Waldheim who, when secretary General of the United Nations, went to Teheran to negotiate the release of hostages. He said, 'I have come as a mediator to work out a compromise.' In translating this phrase, 'mediator' has the connotation of meddling, while 'compromise' had the negative connotation of being compromised. So, according to the story, within an hour of his translated words being on the news, his car was stoned by an angry mob. They responded in what they believed to be an appropriate fashion and stored the event for the future.

Table 5.1 Positive behaviours in negotiation

Summary checklist of positive behaviours in negotiation
• Clarify the end goal and your Best Alternative To a Negotiated Agreement (BATNA) • Take your time – don't be rushed without thinking each step through carefully • Keep calm • Look for opportunities; focus on win-win and only win-lose if you have to • Even in a win-lose, give the opponent an easy way out • Be aware of the process and where you are in it • Use adjournments and different environments to avoid sticking • Don't negotiate when you are over tired • Watch for the other's streetwise tactics

So how do we influence negotiation situations more effectively? Table 5.1 shows some of the important positive behaviours.

Let's explore some of the behaviours in more detail:

Build rapport and avoid irritating the other

Behaviours that build and break rapport are shown in Table 5.2.[2]

Table 5.2 Building and breaking rapport

Words, phrases and tactics used to build and break rapport	
Rapport builders	**Rapport breakers**
• Listening more than talking	• Talking more than listening
• Everyday language	• Using jargon unintelligible to the other
• Adult-to-adult talk	• Parent-to-child talk
• Showing respect	• Disrespectful and dismissive
• Exploring options	• Seeing only one option
• Seeking solutions	• Seeking to impose a view

Our language can contain attitudes that are not always apparent, yet can influence outcomes. Phrases like: 'As of course you will know …', 'May I get your view here…', '… with all your experience, what is your opinion?' all convey acceptance of another person's knowledge and experience. This positive stroke helps to relax the other person, builds their self-esteem and creates a more positive atmosphere. Contrast this with phrases like 'You are not a doctor, you wouldn't understand …' or 'I have a more important meeting right now, could you wait?' These convey superiority and are unlikely to create a positive atmosphere.

Listening

Listening, paradoxically, is one of the most powerful tools for influencing as implied in the old maxim 'If you wish to be understood seek first to understand.' Showing that you have heard the other person takes away the need for them to keep battering away and makes them more amenable to listen to you. 'The cheapest concession to the other side is to let them know you have heard' is another famous maxim of negotiators across the world.

Questioning

Another powerful tool is the use of careful questioning. It helps you gain a true understanding of the other person's interests, especially when you are using open ('Tell me about ...') and probing ('Tell me more about …') questions. In using reflective and summarising questions ('Let me understand what I have heard you say … is this correct?') you clarify what the issues and maybe stumbling blocks are, as well as working at the

2. For a fuller understanding of influencing behaviour, see *Positive Influencing Skills* by Terry Gillen, CIPD, London, 1999.

emotional level to reassure the other party that you want to understand their position and their interests.

Imagine this conversation between a CRO account manager (AM) and a contracts manager (CM):

AM: What do I need to do to secure this business?
CM: Guarantee that you will recruit the right profile and number of patients by the due date.
AM: Do you have any doubts that we can do it?
CM: Yes, given your past track record.
AM: Are we worse than any other CRO?
CM: No, but I still need these patients on time.
AM: Tell me more about what will convince you.
CM: Show me where you have achieved what we want.
AM: So, if I understand you correctly, I need to show you the recruitment plan in detail and a reference site where we have achieved results in the recent past?
CM: Yes.
AM: Great. I now know what I have to do and I will come back to you tomorrow with the information you need.

Some of the most skilful influencers use insight questioning, questions that get the other party to think differently about the problem and which ultimately results in them finding the solution for themselves.

Imagine this dialogue:

AM: So why do you think recruitment of sufficient numbers of patients is going to be a problem?

CM: Because we typically take too long developing study protocols and you are too slow in gearing up the necessary monitoring staff. The end date never shifts so recruitment time is inevitably squeezed in the middle.

AM: So what are the solutions?

CM: Earlier involvement and a better time plan of the process.

Establishing beliefs that positively affect the outcome

Sales people, when they start selling, often encounter a crisis of confidence where they convince themselves they won't get the sale. In order to avoid the risk of disappointment, they fail to ask for the business in the first place and it becomes a self-fulfilling prophecy. Similarly negotiators can convince themselves that it is a hopeless situation and that it is therefore not worth fighting for their interests.

Our beliefs are critical to understanding our motivation and the often unconscious signals we give off. Effective negotiators:

- want to find solutions that meet the needs of all parties;
- are open to other ideas – they don't believe they have the only solution;
- believe that there are common interests, which are best served by striking an agreement.

Use a mixture of pushing and pulling behaviour

Table 5.3 provides a list of pushing and pulling behaviours. Invariably effective negotiators use more pulling behaviour in the earlier stages to build rapport and gain clarity about the other party's needs and interests. Later on, a more assertive (but not aggressive) pushing style might be useful.

Table 5.3 Balancing approaches to negotiation

Balancing substantive and relational aspects of negotiation	
Push	**Pull**
• I propose/want/need	• Questioning and listening
• Challenging	• Thanks
• Probing	• Reassurance
• I disagree/unless ...	• Value ideas/praise
• That's disappointing	• I agree ...
• That's unacceptable	• Summarising
• Deadlines	

Trade concessions with careful consideration of the implications and consequences

According to a Roman proverb, 'He gives twice who gives too soon.' Table 5.4 outlines the key points to consider in order to successfully trade concessions.

SUMMARY AND CONCLUSIONS

In this chapter, I have explored the different approaches to negotiation, namely:

- streetwise tactics
- principled negotiation
- phased trading.

Each approach has its advantages and proponents, but here, to optimise outcomes, I have also suggested a synthesis comprised of the following steps:

1. Prepare thoroughly
2. Open carefully to set the scene and establish rapport

Table 5.4 Successfully trading concessions

Points to consider when trading concessions

- Don't make concessions until you have to.
- Don't get too pushy. Match small options with small options, big with big.
- Don't offer a concession unless the other party makes one first, or unless it is needed to keep the negotiation alive.
- Make concessions in a way that encourages movement and reciprocity, rather than resistance.
- Don't make the steps too big. Don't offer a 10 per cent discount if 5 per cent is refused. What about a 6.5 per cent discount?
- Don't tolerate 'round figures' thinking.
- Don't concede to pressure. Always get a concession in return. (If I do this, then will you...?)
- Give away things of less value than you gain.
- Time is money – payment terms and stage payments, even pre-payments, are often very valuable.
- Clarify your authority limits before the meeting. Only give away what you can afford.
- Call a time-out to refer if you're outside your authority limit.
- Allow the other party a time-out to refer if they're outside their authority limit.
- Be imaginative about packaging. Bundling ingredients allows for tradeoffs.

3. Explore each party's needs and interests
4. Be creative about options and alternatives
5. Use objective criteria to evaluate options and best course of action
6. Clarify agreement at the close to ensure that there are no loose ends or misunderstandings
7. Review relationship and outcomes.

Ultimately, negotiation is about deploying a set of behavioural skills designed to influence an outcome. Building rapport, questioning, listening and getting a balance between assertive pushing behaviour and pulling will all help to achieve the desired end.

REFERENCES

Fisher R. and Ury W. (1999) *Getting to Yes*. London: Random House.
Gillen, T. (1999) *Positive Influencing Skills*. London: CIPD.
Kennedy G. (2001) *Pocket Negotiator*. London: The Economist with Profile Books.

CHAPTER 6

Contract Types

Alan Morgan, *MDS Pharma Services*

The objective of this chapter is to review the alternative methodologies currently being used by pharmaceutical sponsors to contract with vendors, analyse the advantages and disadvantages of the different approaches, and attempt to provide a practical framework which the reader can then adapt for his or her specific needs.

Any type of contract is either explicitly or implicitly linked to an outsourcing philosophy within a company. Understanding what that philosophy represents is an important part of ensuring that the contract meets the needs of both parties and there is goal congruence.

CONTRACT MODELS

Numerous sources have devised a spectrum of descriptive terms to articulate the differences between strategic and tactical outsourcing. The initial focus to this chapter is in reviewing the alternative philosophies of contracting methodologies for the overall CRO fee. These methodologies sit on a continuum as follows and are summarised in Table 6.1:

- catalogue ordering
- insourcing of staff
- fee for service
- fixed unit prices
- fixed price
- fixed-scope risk sharing
- outcomes-based contracting.

When to use each type of contract model will depend on corporate preferences as well as

Table 6.1 Summary of contract methodologies

	Characteristics	*Pros*	*Cons*
Catalogue ordering	Standard materials equipment purchased remotely	• Fast and reliable where the product purchased is standard and quality can be easily measured	• Difficult to measure service or product where specification is bespoke
Insourcing of staff	Specific named staff are supplied on relatively short-term contracts where the vendor accepts the risk of long-term employment	• Deals with short-term peaks and troughs in workload	• Quality of work largely dependent on the individual • Difficult for the vendor to manage and monitor
Fee for service	Hourly rates and appropriate resource levels are agreed but the scope of work is less defined	• Good for start-up and close-down activities	• Where scope of work is defined, there is little incentive for efficient productivity
Fixed unit price	Project is segmented into intuitive units which have agreed prices irrespective of resource used or input time taken	• Budget predictability as scope expands or contracts • Possibly allows vendors to flex resources	• Project management is hard to fit into the model • Vendor has no incentive to mitigate drivers of additional units
Fixed price	Risk shifts from sponsor to vendor within the original scope of the project	• Budget predictability provided overall scope and sponsor deliverables are met	• Tends to be unenforceable because of excess sponsor/vendor inter-dependency
Fixed-scope risk sharing	Risk shifts from sponsor to vendor for specific deliverables within their control and expertise	• Risk transfers to the vendor for tasks within their control and remit	• Number of tasks without inter-dependency is small
Outcomes-based	Risk shifts from sponsor to vendor for virtually all project deliverables	• Almost by definition, the vendor has control of the key dependencies	• Few vendors have the resources or expertise to accept this risk

the type and phase of study, but for all contract models it is critical that there is a clear and unambiguous definition of scope to minimise the risk of disputes later in the project. The scope should include:

- project tasks to be completed;
- clear identification of responsibilities, particularly if more than one vendor is involved; and

- what the expectations are in terms of timeline, particularly for tasks requiring sponsor input.

For example, where the vendor is responsible for provision of a final protocol, the input of the sponsor should also be described clearly. Thus the following timeline might be detailed as in Table 6.2. All parties are then clear about responsibilities, and inter-relationship of responsibilities.

Table 6.2 Clear definition of sponsor and vendor timelines

Task	*Timeline*
Protocol first draft supplied by vendor to sponsor	Day 1
Review and return of consolidated comments by sponsor to vendor	Day 8
Final draft submitted to sponsor	Day 10
Final sign-off by sponsor	Day 12

Catalogue ordering

Catalogue ordering may be best suited to predictable and consistent repeat purchasing and requires no special framework for checks and balances or recourse, since the product is either acceptable or it is obviously not. In the clinical research world this type of purchasing is more typically used for specific products such as packaging materials or central laboratory supplies, but the philosophy has a tendency to seep into more complex service-related products like safety laboratory tests or the provision of specialist equipment such as electronic patient diaries. This approach should be used with care where service is a critical part of the value proposition, because measuring the quality and speed of service is not as easy as validating the integrity of a predictable product.

The basis of costing for these types of contracts is based on a per product, equipment or test cost. This is probably the type of outsourcing best suited to online auction techniques to determine the most competitive price. Contracts should specify agreed deviations from an established quality norm, and address non-compliance. Where this type of outsourcing model is used, it should be relatively easy to measure and monitor quality and other deliverables.

Insourcing of staff

The insourcing of staff from a vendor to a sponsor has developed from the success of the pharma contract sales services, which began in the 1970s. In this case, teams of sales representatives are provided to companies during periods of peak sales activity. This provides flexible resources when activity is at its greatest, and allows the company to reduce resources when activity diminishes. These types of services are now also popular in clinical research and have grown from a relatively small business where gaps in sponsor project teams were filled often on a temporary basis by a few people, to a model whereby whole project teams are supplied to work at sponsor sites under direct sponsor direction. These types of arrangements are relatively new on a large scale in clinical and tend not to be well served by either traditional contracts or established master service agreements (MSAs). Sponsors tend to use this contracting model when they want and are able to exercise total managerial control over the project, and as such, contracts need to recognise the limitations that vendors have in ensuring quality without active supervision under sponsor standard operating procedures (SOPs).

Both MSAs (covered in more detail later in this chapter) and individual contracts are used to document the expectations of both parties to an agreement. Any contract put together for this type of service tends to be based on a 'days/month worked basis' and vendors will typically invoice on a monthly basis, based on the number of staff supplied and the number of days they have worked. Alternatively, some longer-term contracts have agreed a monthly rate for provision of an agreed number of resources over a fixed period, such as 12 months. These types of contracts can also include reconciliation at the end of the period to reflect the actual resources provided.

The fee per insourced staff will comprise a range of items including:

- salary and associated costs
- training
- external management
- IT, for example, provision of laptop, email account, and so on.

Some companies will have a fee structure based on an individual's salary, while others will have bands of daily rates which relate to an individual's experience.

Contracts for insourced staff need to consider a number of items which are not routinely included in typical clinical research contracts. These include reference to staff recruitment legislation, management and appraisal of performance, responsibility for training, insurance cover and so on. In addition, some resources can be specifically named in a contract. This practice can mean extra work if the named resource leaves the company and the contract needs to be amended.

Fee for service

Fee-for-service contracting was the traditional model used in the infancy of outsourcing clinical services to vendors. This type of contract is not dissimilar to that discussed in 'insourcing of staff'. However, it clearly differs in that the resources are under the control of the vendor. The framework for checks and balances is driven by agreeing specific hourly rates on a competitive tender basis and a vendor will propose hourly rates for each type of resource. The hourly rate will reflect:

- the cost of each type of resource including the associated overheads;
- the anticipated utilisation of the resource reflecting vacations, sickness and work loading; and

- the desired margin on the service.

These types of contracts tend to have an estimate of the number of hours to be billed in a given period. In addition, a cap on fees may be included in order to set a maximum fee expected to be billed for the total contract or in a given time period. This contract will normally allow for regular invoicing, often monthly.

The contract should also include details of:

- deliverables
- performance standards
- timelines.

This type of contracting approach is good for initial start-up activities where the exact scope of work has yet to be fully determined by the sponsor, or in close-down activities, where typically if a project is prematurely terminated, the vendor is asked to close down sites or activities as quickly and as economically as possible.

For small and narrowly defined projects, this approach may be useful, but it remains critical that clear expectations of deliverables are set. Few sponsors now feel comfortable in using this methodology for larger, more complex studies because of the unpredictability of the costs, and most likely a suspicion that the vendor will have an internal incentive to over-engineer studies at the sponsor's expense. The absence of a motivation for continual efficiency improvement is a problem for both sponsor and vendor.

Fixed unit price

Fixed unit price contracts break the deliverables into a series of set units such as:

- sites recruited and initiated
- patients dosed
- monitoring visits
- CRF pages processed.

Achieving a sensible balance of the size of the unit is important to avoid bureaucracy and to help manage metrics intuitively. When considering the scope of the project, clearly the big-ticket items are the areas to focus upon in looking at units, for example, monitoring visits.

These types of contract are most appropriately used for projects where there is little inter-dependency between sponsor and vendor in the execution of the task. They are commonly misused where there is significant dependency.

In ensuring that a sponsor can compare competitive bids from alternative vendors it is important that the definition of a unit is made very clear. For example, simply noting a monitoring visit for a clinical study is likely to lead to ambiguity as to whether that includes pre-monitoring preparation, travel time, on-site report completion, and so on.

Establishing a fixed unit price for a monitoring unit really eliminates the need to be concerned about the vendor's policy of charging travel hours (many vendors have different approaches to this) and should provide comfort that if more experienced staff are utilised in delivering the unit then the sponsor is not financially penalised. Other measures to ensure quality are likely to be employed in the contract to, for example, limit the vendor's ability to use less experienced staff to execute the monitoring visit (covered later in this chapter). Clear definition of terms and staffing covenants are the most common approaches to ensuring quality. For example, defining the unit of building a database is of no value unless it has been tested, validated and passed ready to receive trial data.

Currently the most contentious area for this approach is project management, a service which is notoriously difficult to unitise. Traditionally in this model, project management has been unitised on a monthly basis, for example, an average of XX hours a month over a period of YY months. But, although this provides the same assurance around mix of services and cost as a monitoring unit, it is not easy to link to final outcomes and, while agreeing the number of project management units or months provides a good balance of clarity and comfort to both sponsor and vendor, some sponsors are now also employing a percentage cap methodology to limit the total cost of project management units to the total cost of all units.

The use of fixed unit prices enables additional scope changes to be costed without contention, and limits the potential for change orders not directly linked to out-of-scope activity.

This contract model also assists the sponsor with internal earned value calculations. The use of earned value techniques compares at regular intervals in time the actual cost against the budgeted cost of the deliverables produced against the plan. For a fixed unit price contract, the budgeted cost of the deliverable is the unit price agreed in the contract. The plan will schedule when each of these units are expected to occur over the lifetime of the project. Two indices can then be calculated to provide a measure of performance against plan:

- The Cost Performance Index (CPI) compares the actual cost expended against the budgeted cost of the deliverables produced and provides a measure of cost over-run or under-run.

- The Schedule Performance Index (SPI) compares the budget costs of the deliverables produced against the plan and provides a measure of whether the project is running to schedule.

There is an increasing tendency to be very specific in defining specific units (for good reason from both vendor and sponsor), and the inevitable consequence of this is that all processes in executing a particular piece of work need to be mapped to the units defined by a sponsor. Most vendors will have a costing tool that can be adapted to map into specific sponsor units.

The payment schedule ramifications for cash transfer will be considered later in the chapter.

Fixed price

Fixed-price contracts have historically not fixed the scope of projects, and have not been as specific as fixed unit price contracts in breaking down the constituent parts of the costing. This is not an issue if there are not significant scope changes, and it affords the vendor the flexibility to apply whatever resources necessary to achieve the deliverables, with the potential upside of making financial gains if a study can be executed efficiently and/or early. This upside motivation for the vendor is very supportive of achieving sponsor goals within a framework of cost certainty.

These types of contracts are commonly used where the project scope is unlikely to change and the vendor feels confident that the deliverables are achievable. Predictably then, difficulties with fixed-price contracts occur if the scope changes, and there is no clear unit mechanism to agree the costing for those changes.

Fixed-scope risk sharing

Fixed-scope risk sharing is a relatively new term describing a practice of attempting to extrapolate the fixed unit price model to fix the number of units for specific tasks. Risk sharing is somewhat of a misnomer, as in reality this is a mechanism for shifting risk from sponsor to vendor.

For example, vendors may competitively tender for a phase III study where they have each undertaken feasibility work to predict the number of sites necessary to recruit the target patient population based upon the available protocol and understanding of competing studies. The sponsor may invite the vendor not only to fix the unit price of initiating a site and recruiting a patient, but also to fix the number of site units based upon their feasibility work. Depending upon the strength of their feasibility work and the caveat that the key parameters of the protocol are also fixed, some vendors may take the commercial decision to accept the risk that if more sites are needed to be able to recruit the target patient number than their original proposal envisaged, then the cost of initiation of those additional sites will be borne by the vendor.

Outcomes based

Outcomes-based contracting is a further step beyond the fixed-scope risk-sharing model, whereby the vendor may be asked to accept a contract akin to a 'no win, no fee' model adopted by some lawyers. While this model is intellectually attractive to sponsors in that it shifts all risk to vendors, it is very difficult to manage and implement where there are significant inter-relationships in tasks between parties. For example, a sponsor may be responsible for writing or approving the final protocol on a given day within a project plan. Any delay in that protocol release will have a series of consequences to the project plan, which would almost certainly invalidate the fairness of payment based upon only final outcome. Few vendors have been able or willing to accept the risk of true outcomes-based contracts, although they are a constant source of discussion at industry conferences and meetings. For contracts where there are few touch points between vendor and sponsor, as is the case for a virtual biotechnology company, then there is the potential for this type of arrangement to work. In reality, only the largest vendors who have the ability to manage such arrangements with portfolio mitigation would be in a position to accept such a contract.

PAYMENT

Payment terms tend to be an area where vendor and sponsor seek to achieve different outcomes. Vendors seek to receive cash as fast as possible to mitigate borrowings and, in the cases of financially quoted vendors, to demonstrate that there is not a significant gap between revenue recognised and cash received. External financial analysts carefully scrutinise vendors' balance sheets to try and anticipate issues where revenue may have been over-recognised. Since revenue tends to be recognised by most vendors on a percentage of completion methodology, most vendors will seek payment schedules which mirror this as closely as possible.

Many sponsors tend to view payment timings as an additional carrot and stick to achieve project compliance. At their most extreme some outcomes-based contracts sought not to pay the vendor until the final deliverable was made – or made some payments on account contingent and refundable if the final deliverable was not made on time.

There is a disconnect here as most vendors are operationally focused upon being able to recognise revenue (which drives profit and loss and often staff bonuses), while only the treasury department or finance department have an interest in cash payments. To incentivise a vendor, sponsors need to better understand how vendors recognise revenue, and possibly how bonus schemes operate within the vendor company. For example, a sponsor should be aware that if the payment schedule means the project team's annual bonus will be delayed to the following year, there is a significant risk of demotivation and a potential to impact the success of the project.

The most equitable approach is to fully understand the likely timing of how costs will be incurred on a study by a vendor and to establish the starting point of negotiation as cash neutrality; moving away from this point only to establish real performance incentives or to mitigate concerns about the sponsor's ability to pay. Vendors will often ask small biotechnology companies to establish a payment schedule which mitigates their risk of insolvency.

Payment terms for third party costs like shipping or investigator fees should be dealt with separately, and will be covered later in this chapter.

When reviewing contract types, special attention needs to be paid to foreign exchange and inflation risks. Most sponsors will have a preference to be invoiced in a particular currency, while the increasing global nature of studies means that the work and cost base will be incurred in multiple currencies. Most vendors will ask sponsors to either bear this foreign exchange risk, or to hedge for it in the belief that sponsors are in a better position to understand and control the likely timing of payments. Similarly, there is an increasing tendency for long-term projects where it makes sense for there to be arrangements to vary the cost of either charge-out rates or fixed-price units. Some sponsors are uncomfortable with linking inflation to particular indices, in which case the vendor would need to consider blending their costs over the anticipated life of the project. Many sponsors prefer the transparency of agreeing to link prices to independent indices, and are very specific in determining the timing of when that inflation factor can apply.

MASTER SERVICES AGREEMENTS (MSAs)

There is an increasing use of MSAs by sponsors and vendors to pre-agree standard terms and conditions and to speed up contract negotiations. Historically the focus of these agreements has been on dealing with any contentious legal wording issues, and/or to set expectations in respect of payment schedules.

An MSA can be put in place to cover:

- individual studies
- a drug programme covering a number of projects
- a particular time period.

Careful attention is needed to ensure that any work orders executed under the framework of an MSA are project specific and contain an unambiguous scope of work. Alternatively, separate service level agreements (SLAs) can be put in place for each project.

To speed up negotiations and highlight any clauses which may be contentious, a copy of the MSA can be sent out with the Request for Information or Request for Proposal.

SERVICE LEVEL AGREEMENTS

Increasingly MSAs are also being used to set out frameworks for SLAs. SLAs can be written either within the context of a preferred relationship, where macro trends can be reviewed, or on a project-by-project basis. The key objective of the SLA is to summarise the expected operational deliverables and details of the project and/or services being outsourced. The SLA is important for both parties to document the expectations of the relationship.

To be effective, SLAs need to be written within the context of a very precisely written scope of work, where accountabilities are clearly defined. Thus, in the earlier example of understanding the dependency of writing and reviewing a protocol, the SLA for the vendor may state that they will take two working days to finalise the protocol after receipt of the sponsor's comments on the draft.

A typical SLA will include all of the information listed in Table 6.3 and, where there is more than one vendor involved with a project, it is important that the SLAs correlate regarding timelines, responsibilities and deliverables.

Table 6.3 Desired content of a service level agreement

Content of a service level agreement
• Project objectives • Project deliverables • Timelines, overall and to specific task units • Expected resources to be used • Voluntary staff turnover parameters • Responsibilities of both parties • Details of expected communication • Project-specific methodology, processes and systems to be used • Equipment to be used • Key project team contact information • Project budget

In many cases, SLAs are used as a mechanism for holding vendors accountable for key metrics and quality parameters. Typically sponsors will seek to establish SLAs to control vendor staffing. Consider the fixed price unit model; without any staffing covenants it might be possible for a vendor to risk quality on a monitoring unit task by utilising less experienced lower trained staff. While this may ultimately make no difference to the outcome of a project, many sponsors would prefer to mitigate risk by ensuring that staff working on their studies are qualified and experienced to a pre-agreed standard. Examples of staffing SLAs include:

- All staff working on a specific task are to have a minimum of x years' experience.
- Y per cent of units are to be subject to hands-on supervisor review, for example, co-monitoring visit.
- Staff turnover in this area is not to exceed z per cent.
- Vendor cannot reassign staff to other projects without the written approval of the sponsor.
- New staff cannot be assigned to the project (all staff or senior staff) without the written approval of the sponsor.

SLAs can be applied to almost all parts of the project, and clearly establish expectations of minimum standards, which sponsor and vendor agree are critical to managing risk.

Other examples of time-related SLAs include turnaround times for deliverables such as monitoring report completion from monitoring visit and database locks from last patient last visit. The difference between a SLA and a project metric is that SLAs are linked to the contract and therefore any deviation from the SLA will have some form of consequence.

However, like project metrics, performance measures identified in SLAs need to be measured, collected and reported. The administrative burden of measurement needs to be carefully weighted against the usefulness of the information and, although vendors typically assume most of the burden of metric collection, sponsors too need to have sufficient internal resources available to review the data if it is to be of any immediate value. Having fewer performance measures within the SLA tends to reinforce their individual importance as compared to several pages where the vendor finds it difficult to assess the relative importance of each SLA to the sponsor.

Historically, contracts have linked breach of SLAs to an overall breach of the contract. A more practical and equitable approach would be to link SLA performance to bonuses and specific financial penalties.

Contract bonus and penalty clauses

Bonus and penalty clauses have been used by sponsors who seek to drive control over projects. Where used they are often linked to a closing time point, which is itself a very blunt instrument and is unlikely to take account of the project inter-relationships that are necessary to achieve that time point. Linkage to specific SLAs, which themselves need to be clearly defined by accountability, is a more precise methodology. Furthermore, there is a risk that bonus and penalty clauses will drive division between a combined sponsor and vendor team, rather than using a pro-active management style to achieve a common goal.

Some sponsors may seek to link bonus clauses in such a way that the staff working directly on their study will directly benefit from the bonus. This poses a number of challenges for the vendor including the delineation between those included and the support staff who have been part of the team but who are less visible to the sponsor, as well as the broader resourcing challenge of vendor staff not wanting to be assigned to projects where sponsors are not paying targeted employee bonuses.

While bonuses driven directly by sponsors (linked to SLAs or other mechanisms) have issues for vendors, an understanding of how vendors assign bonuses to key staff is important in appreciating the framework of how a study is likely to be managed. Are project leaders awarded bonuses upon change orders or client satisfaction scores?

CHANGE ORDERS

Change orders are consistently an area of tension between vendor and sponsor. Use of the appropriate contracting model and the putting in place of an early authorisation of the scope changes process should address this issue for both parties. Processes to control out-of-scope requests include variations on change-of-scope logs, which need to be authorised by named officers within the sponsor organisation before new work is carried out. Clearly defining the original scope of work in detail as well as clear accountabilities should make this process less controversial.

During the selection process, sponsors often ask vendors what percentage of their revenue is derived from out-of-scope activity. This can be a somewhat unfair and misleading metric, driven by inexperienced sponsors who change the scope of work as the project progresses, or indeed it can be indicative of vendors who bid low to competitively win a study, and then seek to recover margin through change orders. Use of fixed-price units and fixed-scope risk sharing can provide assurance that the value of change orders to the original contract value will be reflective of genuinely unexpected scope changes.

INVESTIGATOR FEES

Investigator fees can represent up to 50 per cent of a clinical project budget, and a number of large sponsors have started to employ specialist teams to review and separately manage this aspect of a project. Many sponsors prefer their vendor to manage investigator identification, qualification, sub-contract negotiation and fee disbursement. In response, some vendors will charge a handling fee for this disbursement, while others will have reflected this charge in their overall costs.

Management of investigators is a critical part of the success of any clinical project and all vendors who work directly with investigator sites need to understand the importance of this relationship.

The materiality of the investigator fee and the complexity of agreeing the fee on a country basis, consistent with ethical committees where appropriate, has driven some sponsors to ask vendors to fix the investigator fee at the time of tendering for the project. To be willing to undertake the risk of fixing a investigator fee the vendor will need to have a comprehensive understanding of the:

- specific therapeutic area
- countries involved
- competing compounds
- likelihood of protocol changes
- financial ability to absorb potential cash losses within a portfolio of fixed investigator fee contracts.

Most vendors would mitigate the risks involved by tendering investigator fees at a higher level than they believe will be actually paid to the investigators to allow for unexpected deviations.

Prompt payment of investigators is an important motivators and a number of sponsors have started to look at SLAs to drive prompt payment for visits or procedures. Many sponsors have provided vendors with cash advances to ensure that investigators are paid quickly. If sponsors are concerned that the vendor may financially benefit from the use of advances, at the very least they should ask vendors to avoid the use of interest-bearing accounts for investigator advances; they should consider the use of escrow, money set aside or deposited with a neutral third party so that it can be used later for its intended purpose.

PASS-THROUGH COSTS

While many vendors are cautious about fixing investigator payments, more are open to fixing associated third party costs such as travel expenses and shipping costs. Expected pass-through costs need to be detailed in the contract. In addition, most sponsors require an estimated budget for these types of costs. Many sponsors seek to control third party costs by requiring detailed receipts and matching them to agreed travel policies. This can be time consuming for both vendor and sponsor, and fixing such costs on a metric such as per investigator visit, can provide control without bureaucracy.

SUB-CONTRACTOR RELATIONSHIPS

For complex studies the vendor may not have internal capacity to provide all of the required services either geographically or technically. Sponsors then need to decide whether to separately sub-contract for these services, or ask the principal vendor to do so. Separate sub-contracting with multiple vendors is preferred by some sponsors who believe that the separate vendors help to police each other and mitigate the risk of project failure. Other sponsors prefer to hold a single vendor responsible for all aspects of the project.

In the event that a principal vendor sub-contracts some services to other organisations, the sponsor should understand whether all of the risk of non-performance of the sub-contractors is being borne by the principal vendor, and most importantly whether any of the agreed SLAs have also been grandfathered to those sub-contractors. In other words, if the main vendor commits to a particular timeline or quality metric, for example, CRF collection timelines, then does the contract that the vendor have with the sub-contractor mirror that commitment. Clarity should be sought as to whether the principal vendor will collect and report consolidated project metrics, as well as the quality control due diligence the vendor has exercised in the selection of the sub-contractor(s). In all circumstances the responsibilities and communication lines need to be clearly defined and understood by all parties.

CONCLUSIONS

This chapter has sought to review the alternative methodologies currently being used by pharmaceutical sponsors to contract with vendors, analyse the advantages and disadvantages of the different approaches, and has attempted to provide a practical framework which the reader can then adapt for his or her specific needs.

There is no substitute for transparency and clarity, and it is also important for sponsor and vendor to clearly understand underlying motivations of specific issues such that goal congruence can be achieved. The ultimate goal is to achieve a balanced working relationship and document the understanding of both parties.

CHAPTER 7

The Contract

Paul Ranson, *Stringer Saul LLP*

This chapter reviews the principles of contract law and then focuses on a typical clinical research contract.

BACKGROUND LAW

Origins of contract law

Before the twentieth century, there were few controls under either civil or common law (see 'Common and Civil Law', below) on what two parties could agree with one another in a legal contract. This laissez-faire attitude was enshrined, for instance, in the French Civil Code as follows: 'Legally made contracts are laws for the parties.' An English judge expressed this principle in common law (see below) terms: 'Public policy requires ... that men of full age and competent understanding shall have the utmost liberty of contracting.' Put simply, this allowed a weaker or poorly advised party to make a bad bargain.

During the twentieth century, most European countries introduced controls, particularly in favour of consumers, aimed at preventing the stronger party from abusing its power. However, even in the twenty-first century, there is still limited protection for parties to a business-to-business transaction, including an outsourcing deal.

Common and civil law

Western contract laws may be divided into two 'families', the civil law of the Continent and the common law of the UK and the US.

The general principles of contract law of the continental countries are mainly to be found in the Civil Codes supplemented by court decisions and statutes. Common law principles are generally judge-made, with limited legislative involvement.

While both systems share the legal values of a market economy, there are important differences between civil and common law. These may be typified by considering the varying attitudes towards each of the concepts of 'consideration' and privity of contract, the good faith principle and how the courts interpret contracts.

Consideration

Under common law, but not civil law, consideration is a critical element of a binding contract whereby a contractual promise is not binding on the promissor unless the promissee gives or does something in return.

Privity of contract

Neither does civil law have a doctrine equivalent to the common law concept of privity of contract whereby a contract cannot confer rights or create obligations on those who are not parties to the contract. However, since the Contract (Rights of Third Parties) Act 1999, a third party is entitled under English law to enforce its rights under certain circumstances unless the contract states to the contrary.

Good faith

It is, however, in attitudes towards good faith in a contract that the greatest contrast between civil law and common law can be found. Civil law has a well-developed doctrine of good faith. For instance, the German Civil Code provides that the parties must perform their duties in accordance with good faith and fair dealing having regard to commercial practices. The German courts have used this provision to set aside unfair contract terms and to create a number of obligations such as a duty to co-operate, to safeguard the other party's interest, to give information and to submit accounts.

In contrast, common law has not historically recognised any general obligation to conform to good faith and fair dealing, fearing that to do so would lead to legal uncertainty. However, there are exceptions particularly in favour of a private individual dealing as a consumer. In addition, the English courts have imposed a strict moral code of conduct in so-called fiduciary or confidential relationships – where one party has placed confidence in the other, such as a beneficiary in a trustee, the person who is trusted may not abuse the confidence of the other party. An outsourcing company and its contractor are not in law considered to have such a fiduciary relationship!

Interpreting a contract

Under common law, what matters is what the reasonable businessperson would understand the contract to mean. If the language clause is unequivocal the courts will not take into account evidence to show that the parties intended something different. In doubtful cases, fairness and reasonableness may play a part, but they cannot be used to contradict a clear contractual clause.

By comparison, under the German Civil Code, contracts are to be interpreted in accordance with good faith and fair dealing having regard to commercial practices, and the circumstances attending the formation of the contract may be taken into consideration. The Civil Codes of the Netherlands, Belgium, France, Italy, Spain and the Nordic countries also have sections on the interpretation of contracts. While the parties' intentions are paramount, it is also provided that interpretation is to be in accordance with good faith and fair dealing.

EU harmonised contract law

Particularly within the EU it is considered that variations between the different national contract laws will impede international trade.

However, initiatives to harmonise the laws relating to contracts in the EU have been somewhat piecemeal and, as yet, there has been no successful initiative to unify the general principles of contract law.

In the business-to-business context, one of the few EU-wide contract laws relates to mandatory terms in contracts between principals and self-employed agents (Directive 86/653). In addition, the EU has established rules which prohibit anti-competitive practices where they could affect EU trade. These rules have limited application to the normal outsourcing arrangement.

There has been a much greater degree of harmonisation in relation to consumer protection. These include laws on doorstep sales (Directive 85/577), consumer credit (Directive 85/102) and unfair terms in consumer contracts (Directive 93/13). In addition, there are numerous employee protection Directives which impose mandatory terms on employment contracts.

However, EU contract law harmonisation efforts continue. In 1989, and again in 1994, the European Parliament passed resolutions requesting a start to be made for the necessary preparatory work on drawing up a European Code of Private Law. The latest proposal on the subject was published in 2003. Given the likely complexity and opposition, it can confidently be predicted that this initiative will not come to fruition soon.

Recognising the wide use of English (common) law as the applicable law in the contract, the remainder of this chapter will address issues in common law. However, it should be noticed that many of these issues apply to both systems.

Making the contract

The law is undemanding as to the formalities required for a contract. Contrary to popular belief, contracts do not generally have to be in writing. They can equally be verbal or even by conduct. As a matter of sensible commercial practice, contracts generally are in writing, but this is not because of a requirement of law.

There are some statutory exceptions to the general principle that contracts do not have to be in writing (including assignments of certain intellectual property rights) but none would seem to be directly applicable to the outsourcing contract.

The requirements for formation of contract are offer and acceptance, the necessary degree of completeness and certainty, consideration and an intention to create legal relations.

Offer and acceptance

A contract entails the transformation of negotiations into a final bargain or deal. The law has to determine when the negotiation process has ceased and the parties have reached finality in their commercial arrangement. A contract is considered to have been reached when a properly constituted offer has been made by one party and accepted by the other.

It is possible to withdraw an offer so long as it has not been accepted, but while the offer continues, it merely has to be accepted by the other party to create a legally binding relationship.

An offer must be definite, and not qualified in any way. In a commercial context, one of the parties might argue that a contract was made arising out of a conversation or exchange of letters or emails. In resolving such an issue, the courts would apply the test: 'Would a reasonable observer have concluded that an offer had been made?'

It is possible to avoid a statement made in correspondence becoming part of a contract by including the words 'subject to contract'. The expression 'subject to contract' is used to ensure that no contract comes into existence until a formal contract is signed. Similarly, letters of intent should clearly state the extent, if at all, to which the letter is intended to bind the parties.

The acceptance must correspond with the offer – in other words there cannot be any discrepancy between what is offered and what is accepted. This can lead to the 'battle of the forms'. This occurs, for example, when one party sends an order on its own form with its own purchase terms and the other business replies attaching its sales terms which do not correspond to the seller's terms. What has happened is that there has been an offer and then a counter-offer, which means that there is no concluded contract.

Completeness and certainty

Contracts must be complete and address essential matters. However, particularly with long-term contracts, it may well be that a particular matter can only be resolved later. While an agreement to agree is not a form of contract recognised by the law, it is enforceable if it is backed by either some mechanism or formula by which such terms may be finalised. Failure of the mechanism should also be considered. For instance, where a clause provides for an outstanding issue to be settled by an arbitrator who must be agreed upon by the parties, what happens if the parties cannot agree on an arbitrator?

An agreement to agree is not to be confused with a contract to make a contract which is legally enforceable if the terms of the second contract are finalised.

Again, a contract to negotiate is also enforceable but would inevitably be of more limited effect as, although both sides would be obliged to negotiate towards the conclusion of a contract, they would not be obliged to succeed.

A contract or clause may be uncertain, that is, it cannot be given a meaning. It may then have to be struck out. If the clause is central to the whole contract, then the whole contract may be declared void. The courts are obviously reluctant to declare a contract void and so they try their best to give some meaning to a clause which is badly drafted.

Consideration

As has already been mentioned (see 'Common and Civil Law', above), for an agreement to be enforceable, each party has to provide some form of consideration. There are rules for establishing whether this consideration is good consideration law but no assessment is made as to its commercial adequacy.

Intention to create legal relations

Parties who are in the process of negotiating a contract use various types of documents, such as memoranda of understanding, heads of contracts or letters of intent. These may or may not be intended to be legally binding. To establish that there is no such intention there must be a very clear and explicit statement to that effect. This is commonly achieved by using the words 'subject to contract' in the correspondence or on any documents which may be used during the negotiating process.

Substance of the contract

We now consider certain the content of the contract. For example, if the parties have engaged in a somewhat vague commercial arrangement it may become necessary to answer questions about exactly what it is they have committed themselves to. In this context we consider negotiation statements, promises, implied terms and exclusion clauses.

Negotiation statements

Many things are said during the negotiations for a contract. Legal consequences may flow from such representations. They may not form part of the contract, but may nevertheless have been an influence in persuading the other party to enter the contract. If these things that were said were incorrect – they were misleading statements or misrepresentations – then there are remedies (either cancellation of the contract – called 'rescission' – and/or damages). Contracts commonly contain 'entire agreement' clauses which attempt to exclude any terms, statements and so on other than those enshrined in the formal, final contract.

Promises

In addition to, and quite apart from, misrepresentations which are not actually part of the contract but which are inducing factors, there may be promises made by one party to the other. If so, the other party will argue that such promises are actually part of the contract and if the promises are not kept then there is a breach of contract. The courts will need to assess whether what was stated was a promise or not. If it is a promise, the court will then need to assess if the promise was part of the contract. The test adopted by the courts is to decide whether a reasonable person, hearing or reading the statement in question, would have considered it to be so.

As discussed above, 'entire agreement' clauses are often included in a contract to ensure that promises made during negotiations cannot become part of the deal.

One should also note the 'parole evidence' rule. This establishes that if the parties have made a formal written document then the courts would normally conclude that the written document is a comprehensive statement of the parties' rights and liabilities. Under the parole evidence rule, evidence outside the signed contract cannot be used to complement, vary or contradict the terms of that document. Exceptionally a party might seek to get around the parole evidence rule by arguing that what was allegedly agreed amounted to a collateral contract, namely a separate contract, which exists alongside the main contract.

Implied terms

Certain terms are considered by law to have been implied in the contract. There are various types of implied terms, for instance covering a point where a contract is simply silent about some important matter. In such a case, either party might ask a court to consider such a gap in the contract. However, courts are generally unwilling to imply such terms except where their need or content is obvious. As indicated above, a court will not imply a term if it contradicts an express term in the contract.

There are also terms implied into contracts by various statutory provisions, particularly in relation to consumer protection. As stated above there are few such provisions in the business-to-business context (see 'EU Harmonised Contract Law', above).

A term may also be implied from custom or trade usage but again such a term cannot conflict with the contract.

Exclusion clauses

Some of the most keenly contested clauses in outsourcing contracts are exclusion or limitation of liability clauses. These clauses are, broadly, risk allocating mechanisms. They envisage the risks that might arise and then allocate that risk.

In ordinary commercial transactions these clauses are a legitimate way of apportioning risk and establishing who should take out insurance against that risk.

The courts have always construed such clauses restrictively against the party seeking to rely on the clause, known as the *contra proferentem* rule. For instance, an exclusion clause can, properly drafted, exclude negligence liability as well as breach of contract liability. But the courts over the years have consistently said that if the person relying on the clause wishes to exclude liability for his or her own negligence, then he or she must generally say so explicitly. Under English law, such clauses can be set aside as unfair but this would only be in exceptional cases where there is considerable bargaining imbalance between the parties. In addition it is not possible for the parties to exclude liability for personal injury or death caused by their negligence and legislation.

Ending the contract

We now consider what happens when things go wrong, commonly because one of the parties has committed a breach. The contract can include a wide variety of other grounds whereby one party can terminate the contract including where the other party has become insolvent or becomes subject to a change in ownership or control.

Any breach gives a potential right to damages (potential, because the claimant must demonstrate actual loss). However, only a 'serious' breach allows the innocent party to terminate. This is self-evidently a somewhat imprecise expression. One test as to what is or is not serious which has been used over the years, and which owes its origins to the sale of goods legislation, is that a breach of a 'condition' (a condition being considered a more critical term) justifies termination whereas a breach of 'warranty' does not.

Another test is to consider what the effect of the breach is rather than what is the particular term which has been broken. A breach which goes to the root of the contract will justify termination.

There are still other approaches. If one party does something or indicates by words that it is essentially repudiating the contract, then this will be allow the other party to terminate the contract.

The parties commonly make it clear in the contract itself which specific breaches justify termination and which do not. For instance, a time clause can be made expressly essential by using the formula of 'time is of the essence'.

If the innocent party is quite clear that it is entitled to terminate for breach, it must decide whether to terminate or not. The innocent party may lose the right to terminate, for example, if it does nothing or indicates in some way that it still wished the contract to continue, notwithstanding the breach. The contract will, however, commonly include a clause to the effect that not complaining about a particular transgression does not amount to a waiver for the future.

When a contract has been terminated for breach, all rights and obligations which have accrued before the moment of termination will generally remain in force and any obligations which would have fallen due after termination do not have to be fulfilled. The contract will commonly state which clauses 'survive' termination.

Damages

Damages are intended to be compensatory – they are supposed to put the innocent party in the same position that he or she would have been in had the contract been properly performed.

The claimant must prove that the breach has caused financial loss of some kind or another. It was noted above that every breach of contract generates a potential right to damages. However, the claimant must be able to show what it has lost. Problems for the claimant may arise if it is impossible to prove what the profit would have been or it may be that an alleged lost opportunity was too speculative to calculate any projected profit.

The other issue relevant to the assessment of contract damages is remoteness. This means that there are certain types of damage, which, though causally related to the defendant's breach, are not claimable by the claimant. In particular the party in breach is only expected to compensate for those losses which were reasonably within its contemplation at the time of the contract as likely to result from failure to perform.

In addition, the party in breach is also not expected to compensate for some types of loss, whether foreseeable or not. Examples include mental anxiety caused by the failure to perform and the cost of executive time spent in minimising the consequences of the breach or in preparing for litigation.

The principle behind damages for breach of contract should place the claimant in the same position which he or she would have been in had the contract been performed properly. This would suggest that the claimant should be compensated for loss of profit.

However, contracting parties will commonly agree to exclude the payment of damages for losses other than direct losses, such as loss of profit or other losses which are considered to be consequential or indirect.

It is always possible for the parties themselves to decide and include in the contract what the measure of damages should be. These are called liquidated damages. The courts will enforce a liquidated damages clause unless the court considered it to be a penalty in which case it would be unenforceable. Broadly, a penalty is a sum which is used as a 'stick' to enforce performance rather than a genuine pre-estimate of damages. The estimate does not have to be precise – provided that it is a reasonable pre-estimate, it will be upheld.

The court has a (rarely exercised) discretion to order specific performance of a contract – an order by the court that the contract should be performed. In outsourcing contracts, such orders would be rare.

Again rarely, a contract may contain a negative stipulation which is broken. The appropriate remedy in such a situation is an injunction. A typical example might be breach of a confidentiality contract whereby an injunction might be sought to prevent unlawful disclosure.

CLINICAL RESEARCH CONTRACTING – AN OVERVIEW

Self-evidently, national practices, laws, and language will lead to local variations. Particularly in the United States, the Food and Drug Administration (FDA) requirements will, for instance, result in provisions that are not found in the European Union.

Heightened legal sensitivity in the United States to issues of liability and litigation risks in general, results in somewhat more detailed contractual documentation relating to such issues than would normally be seen in Europe.

Despite obvious local jurisdictional and practical differences and the absence of any significant degree of EU contract law harmonisation, it is possible to offer general guidance and insight on the current provisions commonly seen in contract research contracts.

General legal issues in outsourcing

Trust

In entering into an outsourcing arrangement, the pharmaceutical company as the sponsor puts itself in a position of having to place a high degree of trust in the contract research organisation (CRO) to act fairly, in the sponsor's interest and to perform to the level that could be expected of the sponsor's own direct employees.

The law has not caught up with outsourcing as a commercial practice. Despite the fact that the sponsor is potentially vulnerable in that the sponsor's business-critical information and systems, together with direct control over and direct access to them, pass from the sponsor to the CRO, the law recognizes no special, fiduciary relationship with or obligation of the CRO (see 'Good Faith', above).

Whole or partial loss of access and control can have serious operational implications. In an extreme case, where the CRO ceases trading through insolvency, the sponsor's business could be severely affected. Legal protection for the sponsor arises only from what is built into the contract; and how the outsourcing arrangements are structured.

Disentangling the relationship

The sponsor must be able to terminate the contract if the arrangements are not operating satisfactorily. It must also be able to bring its contract research function back in-house speedily or transfer it easily to another CRO. The sponsor may be in a dangerously weak position if the contact does not deal adequately with the return of resources and materials from the CRO on termination.

The role of the contract

The onus is on the sponsor to ensure its interests are protected in the contract. The CRO is obliged to do what is specified in the contract, but nothing more. The sponsor must negotiate and demand to include any provisions needed for its own protection or, preferably, to use the sponsor's own contract draft. The sponsor must also take the internal steps necessary to manage the contract and the relationship, to monitor developments, and to have in place contingency arrangements when the unexpected happens.

The positive commercial importance of the contract and contracting process must be recognised and the contract should be viewed and used as a crucial management tool. It should:

- specify accountabilities;
- set aims and objectives;
- specify good performance (standards, quality); and
- establish regular, planned performance monitoring.

The process of negotiating the written contract is a vital opportunity to improve the prospects for a successful implementation and continuing good relationship by clarifying prior understandings and negotiations. This will be facilitated by committing the terms to paper in a logical, structured way, ensuring both sides really do understand each other and what is expected of them, dispelling any prior misconceptions and reviewing pre-contractual planning.

A good contract should cover all of the major aspects of the future relationship with clarity and in sufficient detail. Good, clear commercial contracts improve the prospects considerably for avoiding disputes and successfully implementing the contract.

The sponsor must analyse its contract clinical research requirements and record them with sufficient detail and clarity. The sponsor will incur additional costs if it finds that it requires the CRO to perform further tasks and these other activities are not clearly covered by the contract and included in the contract price.

In addition to analysing contract clinical research needs, future changes to those requirements must be considered and provided for in the contract. Once the necessary contract clinical research services are identified and specified, defining the performance required from the outside organisation in plain, clear and unambiguous terms is critical. Performance standards are indispensable, for instance:

- How much of each particular service must be provided?
- How fast are the services to be provided?
- When are they to be provided?
- How often?

Tendering

It is increasingly common for contract research to be tendered. The sponsor should begin by eliciting expressions of interest. Next, the sponsor should issue a Request for Proposal (RFP), containing an overview of the sponsor's tendering instructions and terms, requirements, and a draft contract (if available), to a number of potential CROs. The RFP might ideally be accompanied by a draft contract. Also, where appropriate, the sponsor should include basic information about the assets and services that the potential new outsourcer will inherit. The bidders should be encouraged to respond to the RFP in the prescribed form, thus allowing the sponsor to concentrate on the technical and commercial differences between the bids. The issue of the RFP should be under strict terms of confidentiality.

Due diligence

The sponsor will wish to perform a due diligence assessment of the CRO. Master contract clinical research contracts are, by their nature, long-term, requiring a significant commitment from the sponsor. This is particularly the case if the sponsor is transferring assets or staff to the CRO. Accordingly, each party will want to satisfy itself that the other is financially sound and can properly perform the terms of the contract. If the CRO goes into liquidation, it could leave the sponsor without critical data, making trials incomplete. If the sponsor fails, the CRO will incur losses arising from the unreimbursed expenses of setting up programmes, acquiring equipment, and taking on staff.

At an early stage, the sponsor will also need to see if the intended CRO is capable of performing to International Conference on Harmonisation Guidelines on Good Cinical Practice (ICH-GCP) and other required standards, and this will require the sponsor to conduct detailed site and facility inspections, and to obtain and verify other client references.

Contractual structure

Difficulties in achieving a formal written contract prior to the start of a clinical trial on a tight timetable, coupled with the problems inherent in letters of intent, have made master contracts increasingly popular. Under a master contract, the ongoing relationship between a sponsor and a CRO is governed by a contract covering all potential projects. Each specific project then requires negotiation only with regard to commercial terms and specific performance criteria, without continually needing to revisit such thorny problems as liability, indemnity, and other potentially troublesome clauses. Master contracts may or may not involve the CRO in continuing obligations between the projects, which might entail fixed payments or minimum levels of business.

Another relatively common outsourcing practice is for the documentation to reflect the distinction between the legal provisions and the precise specification of the services to be provided. Ideally, the detailed statement of the services (commonly referred to as a service level contract or SLA) is attached to the legal documentation as an ancillary document. The SLA should be negotiated by the technical staff, but should be reviewed by the lawyers to ensure general compatibility with the legal contract.

Common terms in a contract research contract

A typical contract research contract will commonly include a range of provisions which may be grouped into the six categories outlined in Table 7.1. Each of these categories is described below.

Table 7.1 Common terms in a typical contract research contract

Common terms in a typical contract research contract
1. Performance terms
2. Financial or commercial terms
3. Data ownership, confidentiality, intellectual property rights and publication
4. Warranties, indemnities, compensation and insurance
5. Termination arrangements and consequences
6. Managing change

Performance terms

Performance terms tend to consist of two types. First, broad provisions covering the quality of the CRO's performance, including:

- Conformity with applicable laws including Directive 2001/20 on clinical trials and ICH-GCP, codes, highest industry standards, and standard operating procedures (SOPs).
- The quality of the CRO's assigned staff and approvals of replacement key staff members.
- Reporting and liaison between the sponsor and the CRO.

A sponsor may wish to ensure that certain general standards of diligence are met. Requirements for the use of 'reasonable efforts', 'best endeavours' or 'commercial best efforts' are thus imposed.

Secondly, there will be provisions to cover the sponsor's specific requirements regarding the services sought from the CRO, together with, if appropriate, performance criteria, estimates, and whether or nor the cost is included in the overall contract price. Such terms will either be in the body of the contract or referred to in an attachment (for example, the service level agreement or SLA).

Commercial terms

There has been a move away from the fixed-fee structure to one based on the performance of individual tasks. This gives the sponsor increased control over the escalation of costs and limits the potential for unpleasant surprises. Special attention must be given to unforeseen costs, for example, those resulting from a change in the scope of the contract and the payment of penalties for delayed performance. While contract law may limit the enforceability of such penalties, sponsors are more frequently seeking such extra sums to cover resulting losses. In addition, many contracts will involve performance incentives – an elementary example of a risk-sharing arrangement.

Invariably, the routine details of invoicing frequency payment terms, and even arrangements for resolving any invoicing disputes will be provided for, as will responsibility for payments to third parties, including investigators and their reimbursement.

Confidentiality, ownership and publication

The contract will confirm the sponsor's ownership of all records relating to the trial, including case report forms (CRFs), and will impose the CRO's minimum retention periods in accordance with legal and ICH-GCP requirements. The return of materials on termination of the contract should also be addressed.

The CRO is usually required to accept that confidential information given to it, or otherwise acquired by it during the course of the project, is the sponsor's property and must be kept confidential. The contract may also require that the CRO impose equivalent obligations on its staff and investigators. 'Confidential information' should be defined in detail sufficient enough that the parties are aware of what is and what is not confidential. The contract will usually provide that all confidential materials be returned to the sponsor at the end of the trial or the termination of the contract and that the confidentiality obligation is intended to survive termination of the contract.

While intellectual property rights (IPRs) are generally unlikely to arise from the outsourcing clinical research, a typical contract confirms that the sponsor shall own all IPRs relating to the drug and the project, arising prior to, or during, the course of the trial. The CRO is usually required to enter into a formal assignment of such rights, as and when required. Typically, the CRO is obliged to disclose any inventions, know-how, copyright materials, and so on, and the sponsor will have a right of access to all data and information, as well as unrestricted rights to use them. The CRO may be obliged to impose back-to-back obligations on investigators, so that IPRs generated by the investigator become the property of the sponsor. The CRO will wish to retain those IPRs in what it regards as its proprietary methodology.

The sponsor will want to reserve control over the timing and content of any publications relating to the project. In particular, treatment of publications on multi-centre studies would need to be addressed. Publication is becoming an increasingly controversial area. Nowadays, investigators will not wish to be constrained from publishing, and a sponsor will commonly allow publication by an investigator subject to a period of review and a further period to file any patent applications. It is still common, however, for sponsors to seek to restrain CROs from issuing any publication.

Warranties, indemnities, compensation and insurance

Investigators and institutions generally expect to receive an indemnity against claims not arising through their negligence. The ICH GCP guidelines provide that (if required by the applicable regulatory requirements) a sponsor is obliged to provide an indemnity for the investigator, except for claims resulting from the investigator's malpractice and/or negligence. The contract commonly provides for an indemnity to be given by the sponsor (either directly or through the CRO) to the institution/investigator against claims for injuries or death caused by the use of the sponsor's product in the clinical trial, provided that the institution/investigator has not been negligent, has followed the protocol, and has notified the sponsor immediately of claims.

It is usual to provide that the sponsor is allowed to take over the conduct of the defence of any claim, and that the institution/investigator will cooperate in the defence. Since the investigator is not a party to the contract research contract, the sponsor may issue a separate letter of indemnity to the institution/investigator, commonly as part of the trial documentation.

As far as the CRO is concerned, a contract will usually provide that the sponsor indemnifies the CRO against any claims made by third parties for injuries and damage caused by the clinical investigation of the sponsor's product, except in the case of negligence, misconduct or breach of contract by the CRO. Again, this indemnity will be subject to the CRO giving prompt notice of any such claim, passing control to the sponsor, and assisting it in the defence. Typically, a contract provides that the CRO will not settle or compromise such a claim without the sponsor's prior written consent.

The sponsor may wish to impose a contract provision stating that the CRO will indemnify the sponsor where liability results from any negligence, act of omission, or breach of contract by the CRO, its employees, or agents.

Indemnity is clearly related to the issue of warranties – contractual promises by one or both parties that they will properly perform key aspects of the contract.

In most contracts, both parties will wish to exclude liability for consequential (indirect) loss, liability for loss of profits, and the like. Given that consequential loss is not a legally recognised term in every jurisdiction, it may be appropriate to define in full what liability is to be excluded (for example, subsequent post-marketing personal injury claims).

The contract may also address the question of insurance. It may provide that one or both parties are obliged to purchase and maintain insurance policies against all claims that may arise during the contract period. The CRO is normally expected to have 'errors and omissions' or equivalent insurance along with other public liability coverage, up to a satisfactory amount, and the sponsor may wish the CRO to confirm or provide evidence of the extent of coverage. The CRO may also be expected to ensure that institutions and investigators themselves are adequately covered.

Termination arrangements and consequences

The grounds for termination of the contract should be set forth clearly in the contract. Typically, a clinical research contract may be terminated in the following circumstances:

- at any time at the sponsor's sole discretion;
- where protocol approval difficulties arise with the appropriate ethics committee or regulatory authority;
- in the event that the CRO becomes insolvent, bankrupt, or enters into liquidation;
- in the event of a material change of management or control of the CRO;
- if a party breaches any of the contract's terms and fails to remedy that breach within a stated period; and/or
- in the event that subject recruitment fails to meet the requirements set out in the contract.

Where the contract is terminated at the sponsor's discretion, the question arises as to what compensation is payable to the CRO. Usually, the contract provides that the CRO will be reimbursed for the cost of all work performed to the date of termination, along with any additional expenses for which the CRO has incurred commercial commitments that cannot be reasonably avoided (for example, if the CRO has also committed to purchasing supplies or equipment).

The sponsor will commonly resist liability for the CRO's lost profits in the event of termination and this can be a controversial issue.

Managing change and dispute resolution

The contract should contain provisions allowing the parties to monitor and review the performance of the other party's contractual obligations.

The flow of information between the parties must also be addressed. The substance and frequency of meetings between the parties, along with an indication of who is expected to attend them, should be specified in the contract. The contract should further provide that minutes be kept to record the understandings between the parties during the course of the relationship.

Contractual change management provisions should therefore cover at least the following elements:

- frequent meetings between the sponsor and the CRO to review the service and address opportunities or improvements;
- formal procedures for changing proposals and how they should be responded to;
- documenting and signing off on an agreed-upon change;
- a requirement that the CRO should not unreasonably withhold its approval of a change.

The contract will also provide that the sponsor and applicable regulatory authorities are entitled to make regular site inspections to relevant study centres and facilities.

Other legal clauses

Commonly known as 'boilerplate', a contract with the CRO typically includes other terms of an administrative nature. The most common of these are listed in Table 7.2 and discussed below.

Table 7.2 Common boilerplate terms in a typical contract research contract

Common boilerplate terms
1. Proper law and dispute resolution
2. Status of the parties
3. Severability
4. Amendment
5. Waiver
6. *Force majeure*
7. Entire contract
8. Notice

- *Proper law and dispute resolution.* The parties should stipulate which jurisdiction is to decide the dispute and which law will apply. Where the parties wish to go to arbitration or use alternative dispute-resolution procedures, these wishes should be specified in detail. To avoid the parties going to court over a dispute without having made proper efforts to resolve the dispute between themselves, the contract might specify a hierarchy of management levels at which disputes should be discussed, as well as timelines for those discussions (often called an escalation clause). Where such dispute-resolution mechanisms fail, the contract could also require expert determination, mediation, or binding arbitration as an alternative to litigation. The contract should be written to ensure that exhaustive efforts are provided to find a solution to the dispute, making litigation or arbitration the very last resort.

- *Status of the parties.* It is usual to provide that nothing in the contract research contract shall constitute a partnership or agency, and that the CRO has no right or authority to enter into any contract or assume any other obligations on behalf of the sponsor.

- *Severability.* If the parties intend to include any liability restrictions or exclusions, it is wise to include a severability provision in the contract, stating that if a liability provision is determined to be illegal or unenforceable by any court, then the remaining provisions will be severable and enforceable as long as the contract does not fail in its essential purpose.

- *Amendment.* The contract should provide that no modification, waiver, alteration, or amendment shall be valid, unless set forth in writing by both parties.

- *Waiver.* It is a common feature of commercial life that one party may agree, perhaps reluctantly, to the request of the other, and promise that he or she will not insist upon performance according to the strict letter of the contract. This arrangement is usually referred to as a waiver. A contract often requires a provision stating that any failure by a party to enforce or strictly require the other to observe and perform any terms of the contract will not constitute a waiver or prejudice any other rights under the contract.

- *Force majeure.* It is usual to provide that neither party will be liable for any loss or damage resulting from its failure or delay in performing its obligations where that failure or delay arises from circumstances beyond the party's control. The party relying on *force majeure* should be required to serve written notice on the other party, providing a detailed estimation of the period that such prevention or delay will continue, and to minimise the disruption.

- *Entire agreement and variations.* As seen in the earlier discussion of incomplete contracts, in order to avoid the problems of misunderstandings arising from negotiations and the question of oral contracts between the parties, it is prudent to provide that the written contract signed by the parties supersedes and cancels all prior contracts, understandings and negotiations in connection with it so to avoid a party bringing action against the other for pre-contractual misrepresentation. The parties will also seek to ensure that a variation to the contract must be made by the parties in writing.

- *Notice.* Where any notice by one party to the other is required, the contract should specify how such notice should be served. If notice can be sent by email or facsimile, it would be prudent to provide that a copy must be sent by post within 24 hours after the email or facsimile has been transmitted.

CHAPTER 8

Strategic Relationship Management

Nadia Turner, *AstraZeneca*

Relationship management represents a significant investment on the part of both the provider and the customer. For the provider, this investment represents a cost of sale and the provider will inherently control its investment according to the return it makes as measured by the volume of business passing between itself and the customer. For the customer, however, the investment is simply a cost and the return needs to be measured in other ways and controlled against those measures. Inevitably, the measures will differ between tactical and strategic sourcing solutions – in a tactical environment the measure may be cost reduction while in a strategic environment, it may be reduced portfolio risk. Nevertheless, the method of control is common – strategic relationship management (SRM).

The apparent disconnect between applying SRM to a tactical sourcing solution is rationalised by understanding that even a tactical sourcing solution should be delivering long-term value that is aligned with Corporate or R&D strategy. The return is therefore important and so the investment is justified. There are, however, circumstances in which SRM may not be appropriate – one view is that if, for example, the outsourcing volume is low, then the returns will most likely be consequently reduced and will not justify the cost of an SRM solution. However, another view is that there are many circumstances where the absolute level of spend is low but the services/deliverables being purchased are of such critical value to the customer that it would be foolish to let them be delivered in an unstructured environment.

Notwithstanding this consideration, a general rule of thumb is that SRM is applied in high volume relationships in which there are multiple transactions emanating from multiple locations in the customer's organisation and where activity is spread across multiple projects or therapy areas. The reasons for this will become clear later in the chapter but it is important to begin the following sections with an understanding that large pharmaceutical companies are more likely to deploy SRM than smaller pharma or biotechnology companies simply because, in the latter, the breadth of activity tends to be more narrow. As a result, relationships with providers tend to be confined to single project teams and are often more intellectually driven.

If we acknowledge that relationships with providers represent a considerable investment, then allowing them to fail unnecessarily simply burns money. Historically, the most likely cause of partnership failure has been that of damaged relationships between the two 'partnering' companies. In this chapter, we will try to provide some insight into ways of preventing such costly failures and maximising the value of SRM to both the service buyer (the customer) and the service provider.

We should also preface this chapter with a working definition of the overall goal of SRM. SRM goes beyond traditional procurement techniques, to ensure that we maximise value for money and minimise risk for both the buyer and the service provider within the context of an overall sourcing or account strategy.

DRIVERS FOR STRATEGIC RELATIONSHIP MANAGEMENT

We recognise four key drivers for SRM:

- overall sourcing strategy
- spend mix
- operating model
- spend leverage.

Overall sourcing strategy

The first driver of SRM must be for the buyer to position it as a fundamental component of an overall sourcing strategy. This strategy will formalise the buyer's long-term direction with regard to what it will resource internally and what it will outsource. After due consideration of the following, it should also identify opportunities for strategic outsourcing:

- decision as to whether to make or buy/disinvest particular activities;
- the specific provider strategy including the characteristics that its chosen suppliers must demonstrate and the types of relationships it expects to have with those suppliers.

The strategy must also be built on a collective understanding and agreement of each buyer's core competencies, each of which can be evaluated against the following criteria:

- the risk/value (or cost/benefit) impact of the activities;
- the buyer's own capability and/or competence in performing the activities under evaluation;

- the available suppliers, in terms of numbers and quality.

Figure 8.1 provides an example of how these criteria could drive 'make versus buy/disinvest decisions'.

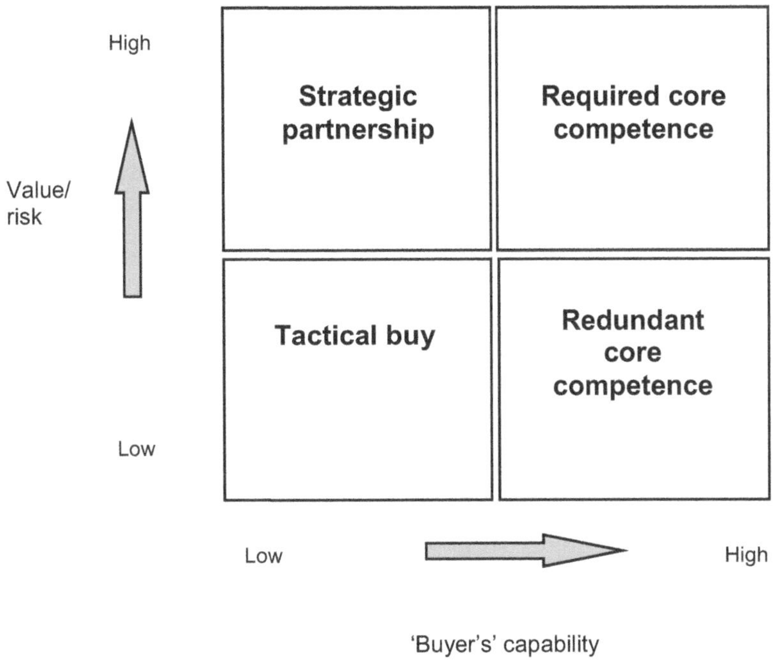

Figure 8.1 Drivers for strategic relationship management: make versus buy/disinvest decisions

Spend mix

Having agreed the sourcing strategy, the second driver of SRM will be mix of spend, that is, the services on which the buyer decides to spend its outsourcing budget. Typically, for the clinical development functions of large pharma companies, this mix of spend will include the following categories of service provider:

- phase I CROs
- phase II-IV CROs
- central laboratories
- cardiac laboratories, interactive voice response systems, imaging and other niche service providers.

Since each of these categories will differ in dimensions such as average contract value, number of transactions per year, scope of contract (size and geography) and legal or financial risk, they require different outsourcing or purchasing competencies, in both management and volume terms.

We have already highlighted some differences between large pharma and the other market sectors such as small/mid-sized pharma and biotechnology with respect to the breadth or 'bandwidth' of transactions in the relationship, but a discussion of spend mix allows us to elaborate further. As we noted, bandwidth tends to be driven by the breadth and depth of a company's portfolio and as the breadth and depth decreases so the bandwidth of the transaction base reduces. However, the scope of activities within each transaction is often wider for transactions in the small/mid-sized and biotechnology sectors. In-house study teams typically tend to be smaller and so more activities are outsourced, for example study design, protocol writing, regulatory submissions and integrated study report preparation are often outsourced by smaller companies but tend to be retained in-house within large pharma. In the smallest, virtual companies, there may be only one or two people responsible for an entire development programme and the primary role of these one or two people will be to manage the provider when the development is outsourced. In addition, small companies tend to have a different mission – they may only be interested in getting a product to proof-of-concept before selling it on to a more established organisation to develop further. Thus, their spend mix will be dominated by phase I and phase IIa studies.

The characteristics of spend mix associated with large pharma and biotech companies are summarised in Table 8.1. Small/mid-sized pharma and larger biotechnology companies tend to sit somewhere between the two.

Table 8.1 Trends in spend mix by pharma sector

	Large pharma	*Biotech*
Transaction base	Wide	Narrow
Scope of each transaction	Narrow	Wide
Trial phases outsourced	All phases	Phases I and II

In terms of more esoteric, early phase activities, such as biomarkers, large pharma tends to develop the methods themselves and then outsource scale-up and routine assay, while the other sectors are increasingly likely to source both development and scale-up externally as the size of the company decreases. In short, there is no panacea, but this is probably just as well, as this would be a one-size-fits-nobody scenario.

Operating model

The third driver for SRM is the customer's operating model and this can be measured, to some degree, as illustrated in Table 8.2. Typical characteristics of a customer's operating model are listed in the left-hand column. By considering the dimensions in the two remaining columns, it is possible to determine the nature of a particular customer's operating model. Thus, if you, as a customer, identify with the majority of dimensions in the central column, you will find yourself driven into a high-cost environment where you need to deploy multiple skills and people to control the boundaries. If, in addition to this, the tasks outsourced to the provider are fragmented across various suppliers, high transaction management costs (discussed fully later in the chapter) are created internally as well as a complex set of boundaries within the provider base.

If, however, you identify with the dimensions in the right-hand column, you will

Table 8.2 Operating model characteristics and potential dimensions

Characteristic	*Dimension 1*	*Dimension 2*
Value drivers	Process	Outcome
Rationale for outsourcing	Access to capacity	Access to best-in-class performance
Corporate culture	Believe you are the best at everything	Open to any means of improving performance
Core competencies	Tactical	Strategic
Operating model	Process driven	Performance driven
Planning and decision-making drivers	Resource gap	Portfolio management

develop a cost-effective environment with deployment of key minimal skill sets to control the boundaries and minimise the points of interface (and hence cost) with your organisation (in terms of not only people, but also processes and systems). In addition, you will develop a clear line of sight between your outsourcing strategy and your corporate or R&D strategy.

Spend leverage

The fourth driver of SRM, probably the one that is considered most often, is spend consolidation or spend leverage. The term 'category management' is also gaining favour as a way of describing the purchasing process that enables such leverage. Spend leverage is most often exemplified by initiatives to consolidate the spend to within a relatively small number of providers and/or to link categories of spend with the same provider. However, if this is not accompanied by a rationalisation of the buyer's operating model, it inevitably becomes problematic to realise the estimated benefits of such consolidation in practical terms. Thus, to optimise spend leverage, buyers need to consider those suppliers whose strategies and business processes are most closely aligned with the buyer's chosen outsourcing categories and operating model.

WHAT DO THE EXPERTS SAY?

As we have seen in the Foreword, the pharmaceutical industry has lagged behind other industries in understanding the strategic benefits of outsourcing. It has also failed to recognise the strategic importance of supplier relationship management. It is interesting, therefore, to look at other industries and to note some of the findings of recent surveys conducted by consulting groups to gain some insight into best-in-class supplier relationship management.

In 1999, A.T. Kearney conducted a detailed study assessing excellence in procurement

(Kearney, 1999). Among their varied findings, which are still valid in 2005, was a clear indication that industry leaders were much further ahead of followers in supplier relationship management than in any other area. More specifically it was shown that leaders:

- classify suppliers according to value creation capabilities versus risk, and segment their supply base accordingly;
- focus on developing mutually beneficial value-adding relationships to leverage cost reduction and for innovation support; and
- are prevalent in managing the upside potential of relationships via incentive programmes in contracts.

More recently, in 2003, McKinsey & Company commented that 'Traditional purchasing organisations are involved with infrequent bidding with some suppliers and undemanding "partnerships" with too many. World-class organisations build a supplier network with a few demanding partnerships for goods and services that can truly contribute to competitive advantage' (McKinsey & Co., 2003). In short, it seems that a small number of well-managed and well-developed partnerships has the potential to offer both buyer and supplier with long-term benefits. In 2005 and beyond, these statements still ring true.

However, before moving onto the development of strategic relationships, it seems fitting to mention the top-line findings of a Vantage Partners survey on Alliance Relationship Management conducted in 2001. The output of interviews conducted with more than 150 alliance managers in over 120 companies (all blue chip organisations including large pharma, micro-electronics and automotive sectors) provides clear evidence that there is a strong need to actively and effectively manage relationships. In more than half of all cases, partnership failure was attributed to poor or damaged relationships between customer and supplier (Figure 8.2). The most important factors contributing to the breakdown were:

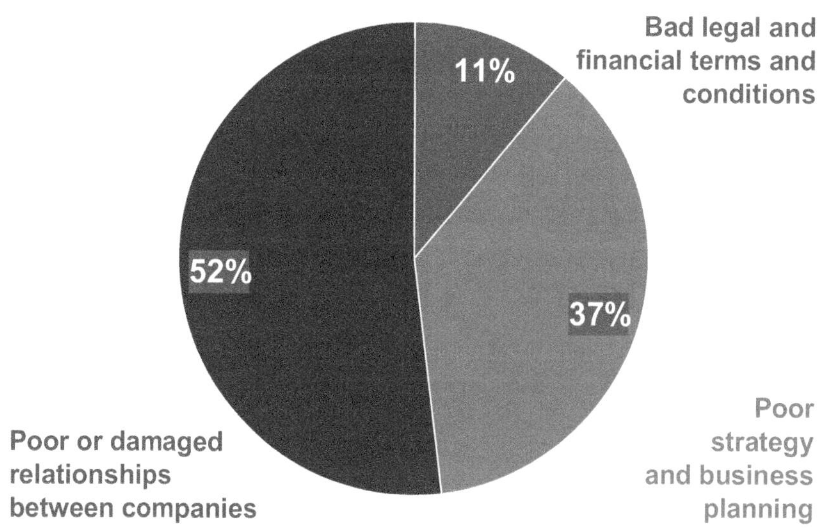

Figure 8.2 The leading causes of partnership failure

Source: Vantage Partners *Alliance Relationship Management* Study 2001

- breakdown in trust
- build-up of negative partisan perceptions
- questioning of one another's motives
- festering conflicts
- little joint problem-solving
- feeling of disrespect and/or of coercion.

SUPPLIER RELATIONSHIP CHARACTERISTICS

Conventional wisdom has suggested that, as demonstrated in Figure 8.3, the concept of the supplier relationship continuum is a necessary evolution.

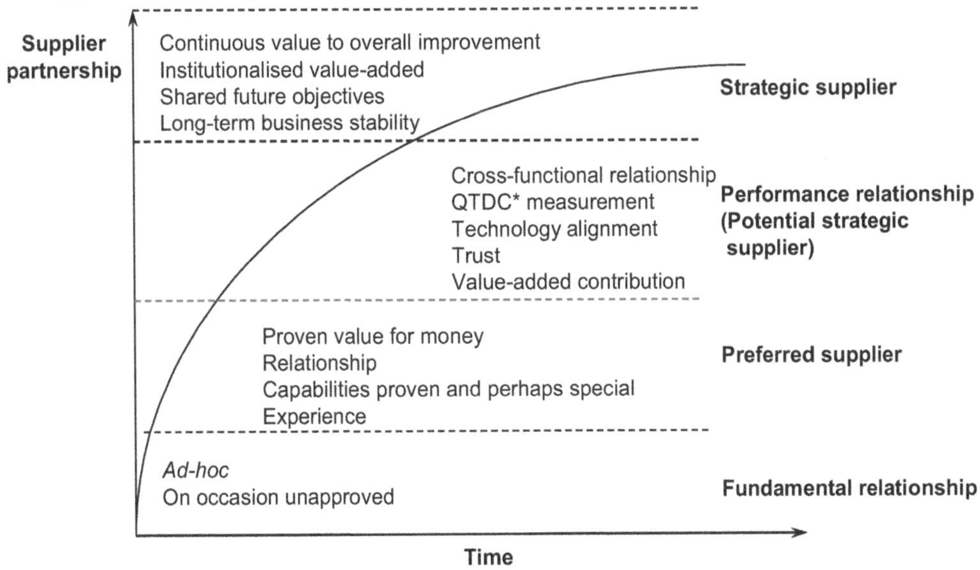

It will take time and evolution to build processes, tools, technology, experience, trust and relationships.
* QTDC = Quality, Time, Delivery, Cost

Figure 8.3 Supplier relationship continuum

However, we can perhaps challenge this assumption. Figure 8.4 illustrates that there are many different levels of supplier relationship, from transactional through to integration, and that any of these may be valid under the right circumstances and, therefore, should be sought after in its own right. Thus, we should not necessarily be trying to move all relationships from the transactional to the strategic mode without first making reference to the sourcing strategy and the required supplier characteristics and relationships as mentioned earlier in the chapter. In addition, these levels can all legitimately exist across the spectrum of transactions with a particular provider and the SRM strategy should be flexible enough to manage any or all of them. However, it would be true to say that if a strategic relationship is sought, this would typically be developed through the continuum stages.

Moving on to the characteristics of 'high performing' relationships or alliances, Figure 8.5 provides an overview of how this should work from the perspective of both the customer

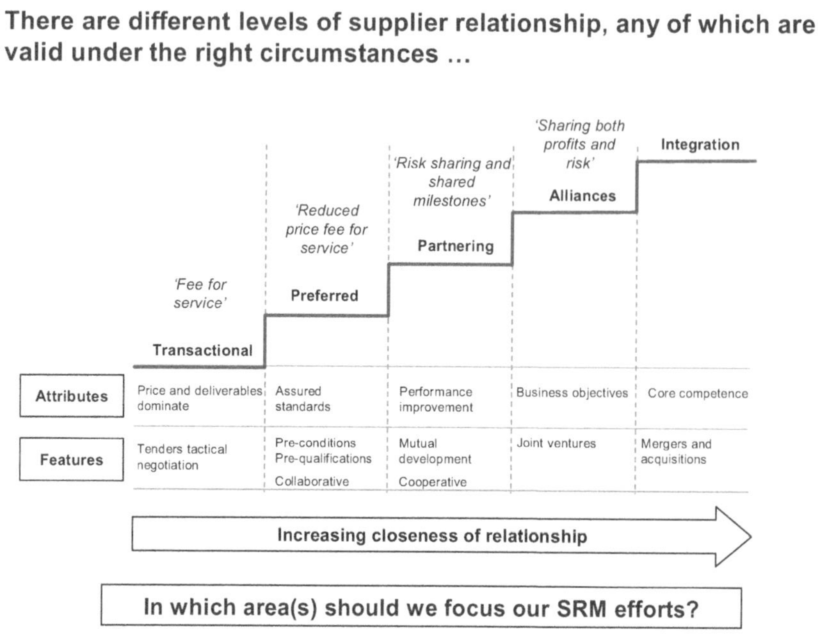

and the provider.

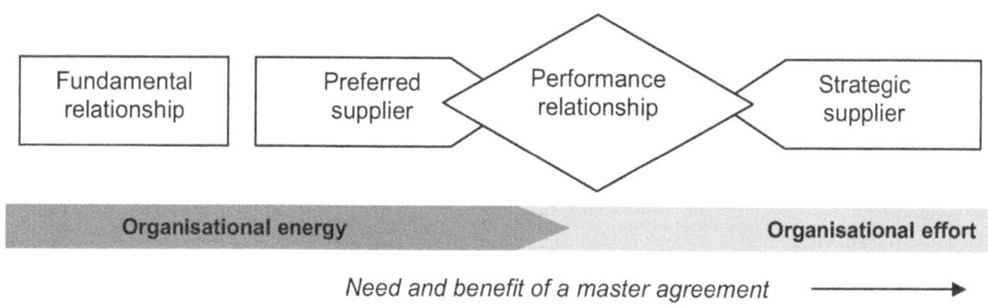

Culture	
Compatibility	Positively supports its mission, key values and goals
Attitude and commitment	Alliance participants must have a common sense of purpose
Managed trust	The most important competency fostered at all levels
Equity	Equal contribution of resources in relation to benefits
Performance incentives	KPIs should be agreed by both parties
Management	
Functional capabilities	Appropriate use of each party's capabilities to optimise alliance performance
Strategic consistency	Common and mutually dependent objectives
Process	
Good client behaviour	Alliance participants treat each other's people as if they were their own
Information sharing	Open, blame-free and quick communications

Figure 8.4 Supplier relationship levels
Figure 8.5 Characteristics of high-performing alliances

It is perhaps worth noting that the expectation, as we move from a fundamental or tactical relationship to the strategic dimension, is that the organisational effort, measured mainly in terms of full-time equivalents (FTEs), should reduce whereas the energy or value output should increase, measured in terms of both FTEs and dollars.

PRINCIPLES OF SRM

The three key dimensions of SRM are illustrated in Figure 8.6. The project or study manager is responsible for managing the specific project or work order deliverables. The technical standards are developed and managed at a 'supra-project' or project-independent level and are monitored by the buyer's technical specialists. The business and relationship aspects of the project are managed at a project level by an outsourcing/purchasing specialist but are then managed at the supra-project level by the strategic relationship manager or account manager.

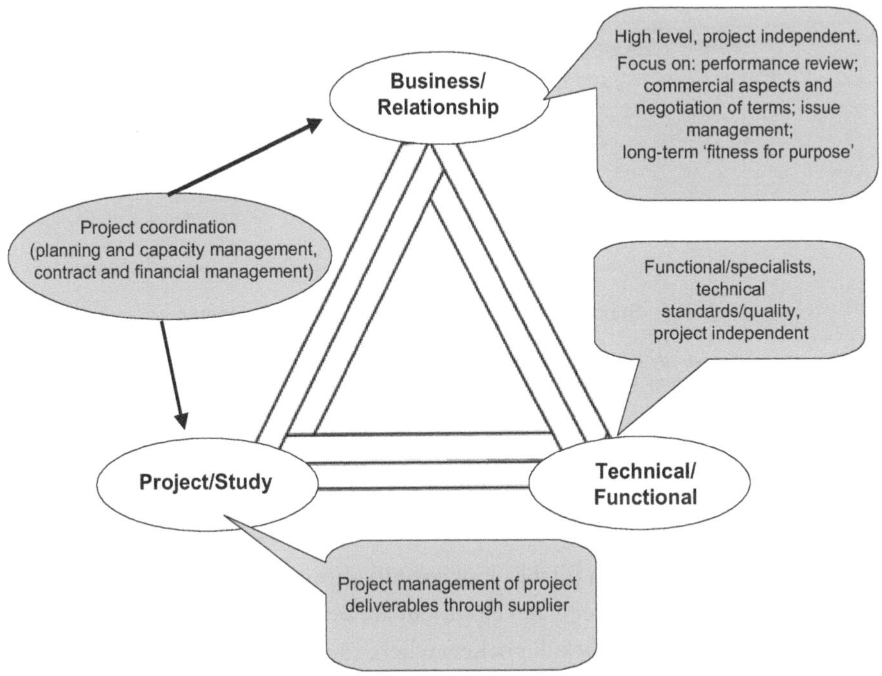

Figure 8.6 Principles of supplier management

Typically, the service provider would mirror the SRM role with an equivalent account director or executive role. As well as aspects of performance management, both account managers would assume accountability for the appropriate application of corporate governance, that is, proper accountability, integrity and openness in the conduct of their organisation's business, to the relationship. This latter accountability has taken on a much greater significance since the Sarbanes-Oxley Act of 2002 introduced significant legislative changes to financial practice and corporate governance regulation including rules which are aimed at protecting investors by improving the accuracy and reliability of corporate disclosures made pursuant to securities laws in the United States.

RELATIONSHIP STRUCTURES

The transition from the base case of project managers running contracts and provider relationships directly, to full-scale SRM naturally follows a continuum. The first progression tends to be the introduction of contract management as a function – going forward this will be an increasingly important first step in order to meet the evolving governance requirements placed on companies traded publicly in the US. This initial phase ensures that appropriate skills are deployed against (presumably) growing levels of spend and is therefore a critical evolution, but it may also begin to create the 'chaos' of multiple touch points between customer and provider as highlighted in Figure 8.7.

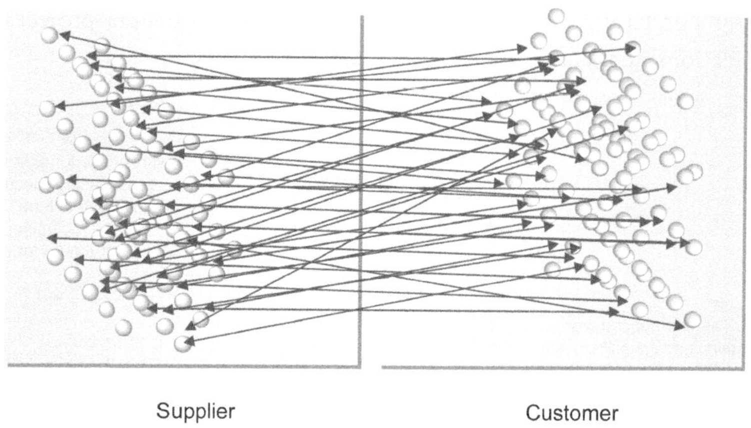

Everybody talks to each other. No co-ordination, no relationship structure, no strategy development. Big danger of reinventing the wheel many times.

Figure 8.7 Chaotic relationship structure

We may hope that the days of a total lack of coordination within the relationship structure in the absence of strategic development are behind us. However, within large organisations, there are probably still pockets where such chaos exists and we therefore need to recognise the resulting relationship structure (Figure 8.7). It is perhaps obvious to point out that in this scenario there is a grave danger that the overall cost of maintaining the relationship, in terms of time, money and resource, will outweigh the potential benefits of working with the service provider. In this situation, many organisations will have recognised the need to evolve the relationship structure and, today, the most typical relationship structure is probably that depicted in Figure 8.8.

We can immediately see, however, that although the communication pathways shown in Figure 8.8 are much more simple than in Figure 8.7, the set-up does not provide scope to maximise the value that both parties can bring to the table. In addition, the single point of contact can easily result in a communication bottleneck.

Instead, we should be evaluating the structure which, for now at least, represents best practice in SRM, namely *key account management*. The principles of key account

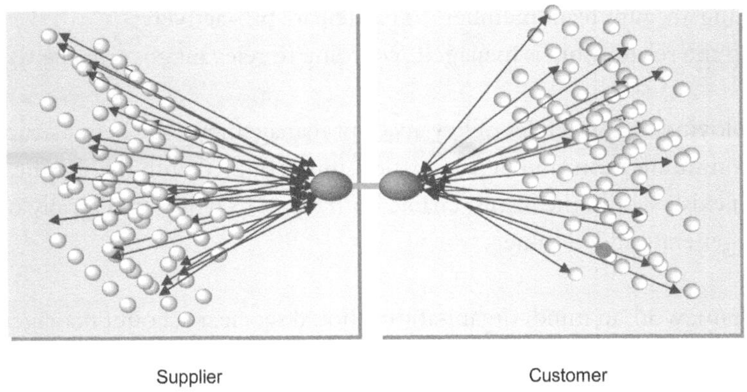

Probably the most typical relationship structure seen today. Expertise on both sides is seriously under-utilised. Both sides are expected to be all-round experts. Information is translated along the chain: expert to non-expert to non-expert to expert.

Figure 8.8 Relationship structure typically seen in 2005

management should be relevant to all customer types, be they small or large pharma companies. However, in practice, it is typically larger organisations which are putting this structure in place.

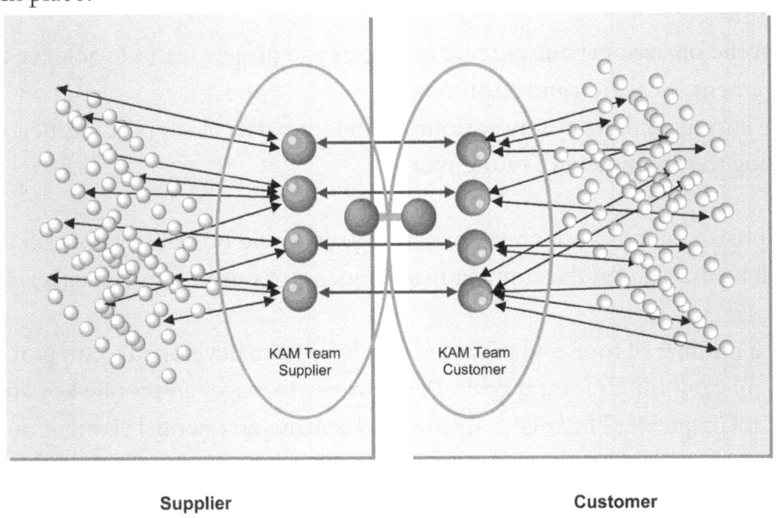

Structured and better managed communication and relationship through the Key Account Manager (KAM) and multi-functional team. Lots of know-how within the teams enable both teams to work strategically on joint projects to generate added value.

Figure 8.9 Key account management structure

In this set-up, shown in Figure 8.9, the key account managers from both the customer and supplier are responsible for:

- managing the overall customer/supplier relationship;
- managing the relationship structure and development and coordinating members of the account teams across each of the various disciplines;
- developing and managing a continuous improvement process that will create value for both the customer and supplier;

- motivating account team members to participate pro-actively;
- ensuring the relationship is managed according to relevant governance requirements.

When employing the principles of key account management, the better structured and managed communication, and hence relationships, coupled with the significant know-how which exists within the teams, enable both teams to work strategically on joint projects to generate added value.

With this framework in mind, organisations should set clear account management goals and, to be truly effective, these should be communicated between the customer and supplier and steps taken to ensure all parties understand them. In practice, for a large pharma organisation, such goals would include:

- provide account oversight to maximise the value of preferred and/or strategic partner arrangements and/or relationships;
- manage a volume of business that is consistent with the desired account goals for the provider;
- identify and potentially resolve trends and issues across the project portfolio;
- champion and build the value-adding nature of preferred and strategic relationships to the business;
- support the operational outsourcing managers and project teams to achieve issue management, escalation and resolution;
- analyse current and prospective resource utilisation data to support business decisions regarding the assignment of future work.

For small pharma and biotech companies, the goals would be similar although the process might well be managed at the contract management (or outsourcing manager) level.

There are a number of tools and processes that have been developed to support account management responsibilities and goals. Performance management is one key area and is discussed in Chapter 9. The balanced scorecard remains an essential element in the account managers' tool-box and should form the basis of any periodic formal review meetings held between the customer and supplier. Such review meetings may take the form of a supplier forum, an open meeting involving both customer and supplier representatives, where reviews are conducted across the project portfolio to facilitate trend identification and resolution. In addition, for the most part, supplier forums will:

- provide an arena for suppliers to have dialogue with customers at both the team and senior levels;
- encourage mutual understanding of roles and responsibilities, goals and objectives;
- discourage 'corridor talk', or at least reduce its impact, and share knowledge based on objective metrics, surveys, lessons learned and end of project meetings; and
- raise the profile of the supplier and of outsourcing *per se* within the customer organisation.

It is important that these events produce tangible outputs, that is, benefits and actions that are then communicated to all invitees and stakeholders and are tracked and reported regularly to both customer and supplier. The responsibility for this activity would normally fall under the remit of the account manager.

Supplier forums should be held periodically at a frequency that depends on the volume and scope of portfolio, but at least once a year. It is also recommended that the customer–supplier relationship is reviewed strategically at regular intervals. This strategic review would be the key objective of a business review meeting and would typically also be facilitated by the account manager. Key senior stakeholders from both the customer, for example, the Head of Outsourcing plus a key senior member of the project community for whom the supplier is providing a significant service, and the supplier, for example, the Strategic Relationship Manager plus a senior operations manager, would take part in the meeting. The objectives of the review meeting should include:

- A review of the current portfolio including high-level review of current projects with particular emphasis on the status of projects which are of particular or strategic importance.

- A review of the overall status of the relationship at the highest level. Thus, if the relationship is global, the review must have a global perspective and cover all service areas and should make full use of available metrics and performance information including, for example, the balanced scorecard, supplier forum outputs and the account manager's own overview of performance. This would include obtaining feedback from the suplier on the customer's performance, and how changes could benefit the relationship.

- A discussion of current and potential pricing and any discounting arrangements.

- A discussion and alignment of partnership expectations and goals, both at present and in the future.

- A review of the likely potential portfolio moving forward and the strategic options to deliver it.

In terms of alignment of partnership goals and expectations, another tool at the disposal of the account manager (for both customer and supplier) is the account plan. This should be built and maintained to contain all key information pertaining to the account, such as financial and revenue information, project and performance reviews, resource utilisation data, opportunity tracking and so on, as well as a clear set of objectives for development of the account. In a performance-driven relationship, appropriate communication of the respective account plans and objectives among customer and supplier personnel is key to increasing transparency and aligning goals as far as possible.

TRANSACTION MANAGEMENT COSTS

Total cost of ownership (TCO) is a well-known concept within the purchasing communities of the pharmaceutical industry. The price paid to the supplier represents a major portion, but not the total cost of outsourcing. The TCO needs to also take into account the internal/incremental costs for:

- relationship management
- project management
- interfaces, for example, systems
- changes, performance deviations and late delivery.

Transaction management costs (TMCs) are one component of the overall TCO framework and represent the costs of the in-house resources that customer organisations are required to invest in order to manage their third party providers. Thus, these would typically include the costs highlighted in the first two bullets above.

Measuring transaction management costs

Customers need to be able to reliably measure the TMCs associated with their chosen operating model and there are two basic ratios that can be used to do this.

- The ratio of average annual number of FTEs deployed at the supplier to the average annual number of customer FTEs deployed in-house, that is, supplier FTEs: sponsor FTEs.

- The ratio of the average annual supplier costs (service fees only) for the project to the average annual cost of the customer resource deployed to manage execution by the supplier, that is, the annual customer cost divided by the supplier professional fees for the same period expressed as cents/dollar.

External benchmarks

There are no formal benchmarks available for TMCs in the pharmaceutical industry but anecdotal evidence from many of the larger service providers suggests that most large pharma customers incur TMCs of 30–40 cents in the dollar. The biotechnology sector inevitably runs with a more minimalist operating model and as a result incurs TMCs closer to 15 cents in the dollar. However, in other industries the evidence of efficiencies is clear, and information systems outsourcing, which represents a much more mature model, operates with TMCs of just four cents in the dollar.

Potential benefits of reduced transaction management costs

The potential financial benefits of reducing TMCs are highly significant. The pharmaceutical and biotechnology industry as a whole spends approximately $10 bn each year on contract clinical service provision (Graham Hughes, 2003). Assuming that half of this sum is spent by large pharma, and that the average rate of TMCs for large pharma is in the region of 35 cents/$, then each year large pharma consumes more than $1.75 bn of internal resource in managing that spend.

Furthermore, if large pharma could reduce TMCs by 25 per cent, then annual savings of more than $400 m for the industry as a whole might be achieved. Individual companies have only to extrapolate this estimate to their own annual outsourcing spend to gain an understanding of the potential impact similar efficiencies might have on their own bottom line.

Inevitably, implementing a key account management system has the potential, initially at least, to increase overall TMCs since account managers are incremental in resource terms to the existing transaction or outsourcing management team. It is therefore critical to ensure that the return on leverage of that spend is of sufficient volume to justify the investment.

LESSONS LEARNED

The concept of SRM is still relatively new to the pharmaceutical industry, at least at the level of the customer, and consequently, we face a number of challenges as the concept and practice starts to embed within, in particular, large pharma organisations. Fortunately though, as practices change, we have the opportunity to rapidly learn lessons and adapt our behaviour accordingly. AstraZeneca has been trying to apply the concept of SRM in clinical development since mid-2002 and although our experience is that of a large pharmaceutical company outsourcing services on a global scale, it is useful to share some of the topline lessons that we have learned.

- The supplier strategy must be reviewed along with the reality of the portfolio and business demands, such as productivity targets.
- The role of the account manager and the target benefits of SRM must be clearly defined and communicated to all stakeholders, both at the outset and periodically as the process is developing.
- The account manager walks a difficult tight-rope where he or she needs to be seen as a fair advocate for their provider and not as a salesperson for that provider.
- The account manager will have limited strategic influence and/or input if the planning horizon for work allocation is, as is often the case, too short. The account manager should be afforded the opportunity to influence the outsourcing strategy and operating model to facilitate strategic planning with their provider.
- The SRM process should incorporate a process for supplier de-selection as well as selection. This should be a documented transparent process underpinned by the performance management process.
- Notwithstanding all of the tools, processes and governance that must exist in SRM, personal chemistry and individual relationships between customers and suppliers are still very important and their influence should not be underestimated.

SUMMARY

Although SRM is gaining credibility and momentum across the pharmaceutical industry, it is still a relatively new concept. The key drivers for SRM, that is, sourcing strategy, spend mix, operating model and spend leverage, should ideally be adequately understood ahead of implementing a SRM strategy. Evidence suggests that failure to address SRM adequately results in failure to realise the true benefits of strategic outsourcing. Strategic relationships are built through evolution although each stage of the evolution can be a desirable state in its own right.

SRM has three key dimensions that should be considered and managed throughout:

- project deliverables
- technical specifications and performance standards
- the business/relationship dimension.

Key account management represents current best practice in SRM, and the account manager must marry performance, risk and relationship management in order to achieve the desired SRM objectives. The industry should also address the issue of reducing its TMCs, the cost of managing third party providers, where there are significant cost and efficiency gains to be realised and, as SRM develops within the industry, learning will need to be captured, shared and actioned if we are to realise the potential benefits of SRM.

The pharmaceutical industry has been under pressure for a number of years to increase productivity and reduce costs and there are no signs of this pressure abating. SRM is one step towards improving the manner in which we procure services and the relative success of that process. However, although the title of this chapter is 'Strategic Relationship Management', it is clear that we are moving to an environment where our focus will shift again, this time from managing relationships to managing accounts.

REFERENCES

Graham Hughes R. (2003) *European Pharmaceutical Contractor.* The CRO Scene 2003, pp. 8–10.

Kearney A.T. (1999) *Assessment on Excellence in Procurement.* A.T. Kearney.

McKinsey & Co. (2003) *World Class Purchasing and Supply Management.* Module 1 Training within AstraZeneca.

Sarbanes-Oxley Act (2002) 107th Congress of United States of America, 2nd Session, 23 January.

Weiss, J., Ertel, D. and Visiori, L.J (2001) *Managing Alliance Relationships – A Cross-industry Study of How to Build and Manage Successful Alliances.* Boston, MA and Los Angeles, CA: Vantage Partners.

CHAPTER 9

Performance Management

Michelle Cuddigan and Sarah King, *IBM Business Consulting Services*

When you can measure what you are speaking about, and express it in numbers, you know something about it; but when you cannot measure it, when you cannot express it in numbers, your knowledge is of a meager and unsatisfactory kind.
William Thompson (Lord Kelvin)

Estimated 2004 expenditure[1] on outsourced CRO services (Phases I-IV) was some $9.4 bn. This represented 22.2 per cent of total estimated pharma R&D expenditure and the figure is forecast to grow by 14.6 per cent per annum to 2007. One of the major factors in the anticipated continued growth of the CRO sector is the increasing number of biotech players in the R&D area and the fact that most of these cannot and do not intend to develop the level of internal clinical development resources of their larger competitors.

Constrained budgets and sparse R&D pipelines amongst many of the industry players means that outsourcing dollars are now scrutinised more than ever to ensure that the maximal value is extracted from this spend. However, our understanding of value is poor and the ability to manage CRO performance remains a challenge for most sponsors. Relationships are frequently characterised by frustration, disappointment and a sense of disempowerment on both sides. There is growing recognition at senior levels of most companies that CRO relationships can be as important as R&D alliances, and that they have many common issues. One of the main reasons cited for not measuring key performance indicators (KPIs) that may be considered useful within alliances is the

1. Goldman Sachs (2003), *A New Global Pharma Outsourcing Market Model to 2007.*

perceived complexity of measurement,[2] and it is true that, with the exception of contract cost and timeline data, useful quantitative data can be hard to come by. However, the data do often exist, and with adequate planning they can be extracted and used to monitor performance throughout the project/study lifecycle.

This chapter will set out some of the challenges, their root causes and some guidelines for performance management of outsourced work.

WHAT IS PERFORMANCE MANAGEMENT?

One of the first points to clarify is what we mean by performance management. One working definition is that performance management is:

A structured approach to linking strategy and performance measurement to concrete actions, with the aim of positively influencing the success of the strategy implementation – thus improving business performance.

Performance management is therefore a tool that will increase the chance of a successful outcome to a project, contract or other piece of work to which it is applied.

PERFORMANCE MANAGEMENT: SOME KEY POINTS

The following list outlines our basic premise for performance management and provides the framework against which we will discuss performance management throughout the remainder of this chapter.

- Performance management is the responsibility of *both* sponsor and CRO.
- Performance management tools should be applied to all types of outsourcing contracts and CRO services.
- Performance management should use existing management information where possible; the process should not consume excessive resources from either sponsor or CRO.
- Performance management is an ongoing process throughout any contract/outsourcing relationship; a post-project review is too late to address most performance issues.
- The performance management process should be solution-driven, and should not focus on criticising 'poor' performance.

2. IBM Institute for Business Value (2003), *A Survey of Strategic Licensing Practices in the Pharmaceutical Industry.*

WHAT IS A SUCCESSFULLY MANAGED CONTRACT?

In general, contracts can be deemed to be successfully managed if the following are true:

- Project delivery is as anticipated and jointly agreed by sponsor and CRO.
- Both sponsor and CRO fulfil their obligations under the contract, to the agreed timelines.
- There is no major dispute between sponsor and CRO.

In the context of pharmaceutical outsourcing, performance management provides a framework by which both sponsor and CRO can assess performance against the above criteria, understand reasons for variance and trigger remedial action where needed.

Only by pro-actively managing performance and addressing performance issues, can we expect to maintain the relationships required to competitively execute our development programmes.

WHY DO WE NEED TO MANAGE PERFORMANCE WHEN WORKING WITH CROs?

This question is frequently followed by the words: 'either they will deliver or they won't', or even 'can't we just look at the project budget at the end?'
The over-riding goal of performance management is to ensure and enable good performance and achievement of joint objectives – pro-actively. With this in mind, it is clear that performance must be managed throughout the project, not just reviewed at the end.

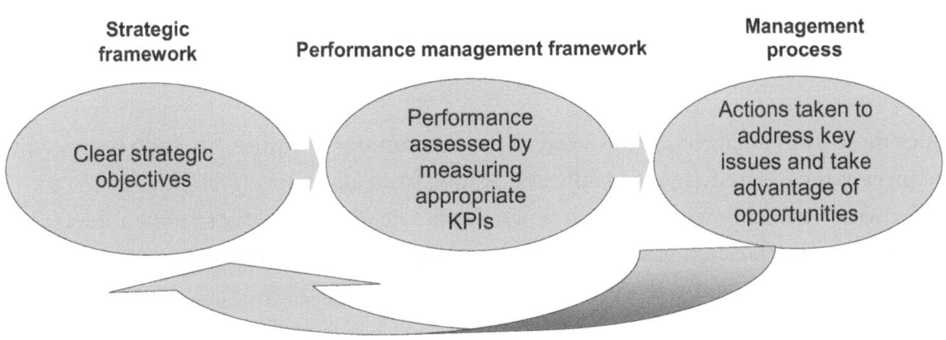

Figure 9.1 Link between performance management and achievement of strategic objectives

Let's think about the stakeholders involved in outsourced projects – that is, the individuals or groups who have an influence on, or are impacted by the project – and the aspects of performance that each can/should control or influence. The list will include:

- Sponsor project manager – accountable for overall project quality and cost. Acts as the principal link between the CRO and sponsor. Ensures that project success criteria are clearly defined with the CRO and that internal (sponsor) expectations are managed. Needs to ensure that outsourced work is of high quality and completed on budget and on time.

- Sponsor team members – responsible for executing the project. Need to be confident that outsourced elements will be delivered to consistent timelines and quality standards.

- CRO project manager – accountable for delivering the project to the standards agreed with client, managing client expectations, and managing internal (CRO) resources cost-effectively.

- CRO project team members – responsible for achieving target quality standards.

- Investigators – can directly impact project progress and/or outcome, for example, by achieving recruitment targets and/or managing data quality at source. Good investigator relationships are key to success.

- Other CRO providers – for example, IVR, clinical trial supplies, ECG services, and so on. Provide data and/or services to ensure overall project objectives are met. Must deliver to whoever is responsible for trial conduct (sponsor and/or other CROs) to agreed targets.

- Outsourcing management (sponsor) – needs to ensure that outsourced work achieves the strategic objectives set out in the global sourcing strategy, where appropriate. Budget and performance targets must be met.

- Client liaison (CRO) – needs to optimise client relationships and satisfaction with the work conducted.

All of these individuals or groups need to have a common purpose – to help ensure that the project is executed as successfully as possible, from all perspectives. A solid performance management approach will meet the needs of all of these stakeholders, and will increase the transparency of performance measures applied to the project.

PERFORMANCE MANAGEMENT: SOME DEFINITIONS

Several terms are used when discussing performance – KPIs, metrics, targets, triggers, and so on. However, the implied meaning of these terms often varies between individuals and organisations, resulting in parallel discussions in what had been considered a common language. One of the first steps in defining an effective approach to performance management is to establish a common understanding of terms – to define the 'language' to be used. Table 9.1 contains working definitions of key terms.

Table 9.1 Working definitions of key terms used in managing performance

Term	Definition
Metric	A metric is a detailed measure of performance. Metrics will usually measure individual process steps or intermediate outcomes of a process. They are frequently single data points that answer a specific performance question, for example, 'What was the study start-up time?' or 'How did the final project spend compare with budget?' Several metrics may be summarised or 'rolled up' to provide a KPI.
Key performance indicator (KPI)	A key performance indicator is a critical performance measure that provides a single view of performance in a given area. A KPI will: ● be key to the organisation, the project and/or the outsourcing strategy ● be directly related to performance ● indicate a result, pending or actual. A KPI is 'the sum' of a defined set of underlying metrics. An example of a KPI could be '% achievement of contract milestones' by a CRO.
Target	Target refers to the desired performance in a given area and sets out the level of performance (quality and/or delivery) to be achieved.
Action trigger	An actual performance result (metric or KPI) that will 'trigger' some remedial action on the part of sponsor or CRO.

APPROACHES TO PERFORMANCE MANAGEMENT

Managing outsourced contracts is complex. This is not only because of the need to manage across organisational boundaries, but because of the many factors involved in determining a successful outcome to an outsourced project. In general, contracts fall into the following categories:

- Tactical – a project, or part thereof, is outsourced to meet short-term capacity, cost or technological needs. No long-term relationship exists between the parties.

- Strategic – the project, or part thereof, is outsourced as part of a corporate-wide strategy. A mid- to long-term relationship may exist. This may be a preferred provider, alliance or partnership.

The relative advantages and otherwise of the different relationship types are covered elsewhere in this book and are not re-addressed here. Different models of performance review are currently used for different types of outsourcing relationship.

Table 9.2 outlines some approaches currently used to monitor and manage different types of outsourcing contract.

However, it is possible for a robust performance management tool to be applied to all types of outsourcing contract. The precise measures used to manage performance may

Table 9.2 Overview of common approaches to performance management of CRO contracts

Relationship type	*Typical approach to performance management*	*Example performance measures*
Tactical/fee for service	• Adversarial • CRO and sponsor use respective project management systems; inconsistent definitions of performance measures • Measures imposed by sponsor • 'Survive the experience'	• Adherence to project budget • Adherence to project timelines
Tactical – preferred provider	• Less adversarial • Joint agreement of key performance measures • Joint review of performance issues – focus on cost and quality • Performance monitored by project teams and relationship management infrastructure	• Adherence to project budget • Adherence to timelines • Achievement of overall cost targets • Client, investigator and CRO satisfaction
Strategic – partnership	As for preferred provider, plus • Joint process improvement • Incentives for identifying performance enhancements	As for preferred provider, plus • % time/cost savings due to performance enhancements

vary depending on the outsourcing model. For example, strategic measures may not be used at all for tactical/one-off contracts.

OUTLINE PERFORMANCE MANAGEMENT PROCESS

Performance management begins very early in the outsourcing process. Where a formal relationship has been or is being established for the first time, the performance management approach should be detailed in the relationship documents. Where the contract with the CRO is for a single project, study or set of activities, the performance measures to be applied to the work should be set out clearly in the relevant contract material.

Irrespective of the size of the sponsoring organisation and the nature of the CRO agreement, a common process can be followed to define, agree and implement the performance management approach for a given study or project. The main steps are outlined in Figure 9.2.

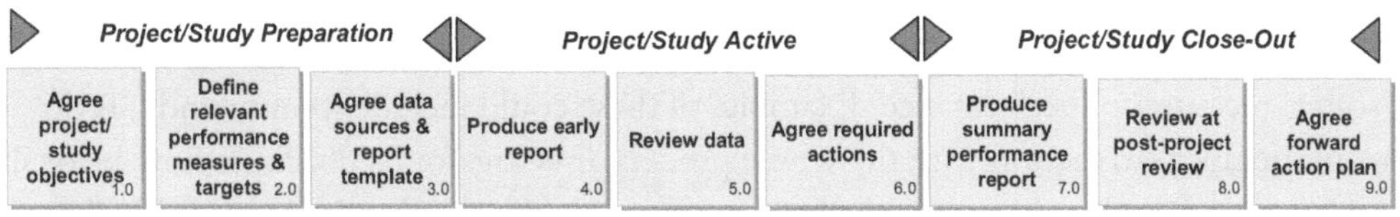

Figure 9.2 Outline performance management process

Project/study preparation

Step 1: Agree project/study objectives

During this first stage, representatives from the sponsor and CRO(s) will convene a meeting to ensure a common understanding of the project/study objectives. Note that these will not only be the scientific objectives; the main focus should be on contract execution so the objectives should be relevant to contract execution. Specific areas to be covered include:

- What are the target timelines and milestones? Are they clearly defined and fully understood by all team members? Are there any key dates (for example, for internal decision points, interim analyses, regulatory discussions, and so on)?
- Who will be responsible for which activities/deliverables?
- What are the communication pathways? (These are particularly important where more than one service provider is being used.)
- What are the quality criteria to be applied to ongoing work and deliverables?
- What is the issue escalation process?
- Are there any process improvement objectives (applies to strategic relationships)?

All objectives should be documented and signed off by the lead sponsor and CRO representatives. Following sign-off, they should be distributed to all sponsor and CRO team members, together with the project plan. The project plan will always include a clearly defined responsibility matrix, outlining relative responsibilities of sponsor and CRO. This is critical since the CRO cannot be held accountable in instances where the sponsor team has failed to deliver as agreed in the project plan. Distribution of the objectives, project plan and responsibility matrix does not have to be a 'heavy' process; it can be done at a pre-study training session or through other communication methods.

Step 2: Define relevant performance measures and targets

In order to ensure buy-in to the performance measures (metrics and KPIs as discussed later in this chapter), the measures should be clearly defined and agreed jointly. Although it is tempting to focus on achievement of project objectives (timelines/milestones) and deliverables, that is, 'hard data', a complete set of KPIs and metrics should include some 'softer' measures of performance. Examples of these could include sponsor and CRO team member satisfaction with the whole process; investigator feedback on how he or she was managed, and/or how effectively learnings were identified and captured. The latter tend, however, to be more commonly used in situations where there is a mid- to long-term relationship between sponsor and CRO.

When defining the measures to be used, it is critical to remember the maxim 'what gets measured gets managed'. CRO resources do not want to be tied up producing complex performance reports using derived data while a busy project or study is ongoing; nor do most sponsors want to pay for this activity. So, we recommend that the measures used are:

- *Relevant* – it should be clear how each metric links with related KPIs.
- *Defined* – a common definition should be agreed and documented.
- *Available* – from existing project management or management information tools.
- *Actionable* – measures should help identify poor performance and/or risk of missing key deliverables or milestones, allowing the team to implement contingency plans as appropriate.

KPIs should be outcomes based. A general guide is that the total number of KPIs should not exceed ten, and in many cases, may be lower. However, the number of underlying metrics will of course exceed this. All metrics must be directly linked with relevant KPIs as shown in Table 9.3.

Table 9.3 Illustration of KPI and linked metrics

Key performance indicator	*Related metrics*
Achievement of key project timelines	• Final protocol to first patient recruited • Patient visit date to lab data transferred to study database • Last patient visit to database lock • Database lock to final study report

One of the most important steps in defining KPIs and linked metrics is the agreement of common definitions of each of the metrics. This step, if conducted correctly, will create real transparency of what is being measured and why. It will also ensure that the correct data sources are used to provide the data once the project or study is underway.

Failure to agree these definitions can lead to two sets of data for the same performance measure. For example, take the metric 'last patient visit to database lock'. A common question raised is: 'which database lock – first or final?' Needless to say, there should only be one (final) database lock! However, if the sponsor is interested in the time to final database lock, but the CRO is counting days to database 'freeze', or some other interim date, the target milestone will not be a common goal. Common definitions of all performance metrics should therefore be agreed at an early stage – to do so later could be construed as changing the ground rules. When defining the metrics, it is also critical to agree what the primary data sources are for each metric. This will ensure that a single common data source is used to report the data, and may minimise risk of conflict later on.

A simple way of doing this is to construct a table expanding on the information contained in Table 9.3. Table 9.4 shows one way of setting out the KPIs, metrics, underlying definitions and data sources, in a way that should be clear to all staff, whether sponsor or CRO. Use of a table such as this should help avoid any ambiguity about what will be measured, why it is being measured, and where the data will come from.

Table 9.4 Example metric definition table

KPI	*Related metrics*	*Definition*	*Data source*
Achievement of key project timelines	• Final protocol to first patient recruited	Number of days from final protocol approval by sponsor to first patient enrolled at first site	Clinical trial management system (CTMS)
	• Visit data to lab data available in database	Average number of days from patient visit to lab data available in CDMS	Clinical data management system (CDMS)
	• Last patient last visit (LPLV) to database lock	Number of days from LPLV at site to database locked	CDMS
	• Database lock to final study report	Number of days between database lock and final approved study report	CTMS
Achievement of target quality standards	• Database error rate	Number of database errors found on database audit/total number of data fields audited	Data manager
	• % non-performing centres	% of sites enrolled that recruit ≤ 1 subject within one month of initiation visit	CTMS
Compliance with agreed contract value	• Final actual contract cost as % of initial contract value	Total project fees after final invoice paid, compared with initial contract value (includes pass-through costs)	Finance
	• Number of change orders	Number of change orders approved after initial contract sign-off	Finance

For each measure, there should also be an assigned data 'owner'. For example, when measuring the percentage of non-performing centres, the data source is likely to be a clinical trial management system (CTMS) and the data owner could be the sponsor or the CRO project manager, depending on whose CTMS is being used.

The final part of this process step is to agree target performance levels for each of the metrics to be measured. These should be documented by again building on the KPI/metric table as shown in Table 9.5.

Table 9.5 Illustration of performance targets linked to KPIs and individual metrics

KPI (example)	*Related metrics*	*Definition*	*Data source*	*Target**
Achievement of key project timelines	• Final protocol to first patient recruited	Number of days from final protocol approval by sponsor to first patient enrolled at first site	CTMS	60 days (mean); 90 days (oncology)
	• Visit data to lab data available in database	Average number of days from patient visit to lab data available in CDMS	CDMS	5 days
	• LPLV to database lock	Number of days from LPLV at last site to database locked	CDMS	5 days
	• Database lock to final study report	Number of days between database lock and final approved study report	CTMS	21 days

* All days specified are elapsed time

One critical point to remember at this stage is that targets set for work conducted by CROs should be broadly consistent with targets set for internal project teams. In other words, you should not set higher expectations for CROs unless they have specifically agreed to them!

Step 3: Agree reporting template

The final step at the pre-study stage is to agree the reporting template. This will differ by sponsor and CRO. Some CROs have performance tools that allow customised print-outs of the relevant performance measures, and some sponsors require a specific format. The precise template will depend on the tool being used; a balanced scorecard tool, for example, will usually provide a formatted report. Example templates will be provided later in the chapter when we discuss performance management tools.

During the active phase of the project/study

Step 4: Produce an early report

Status reports will normally be produced monthly or quarterly, depending on the project. However, it is useful to produce an early report of agreed performance measures within one month or six weeks of contract start. The sponsor project manager will normally be

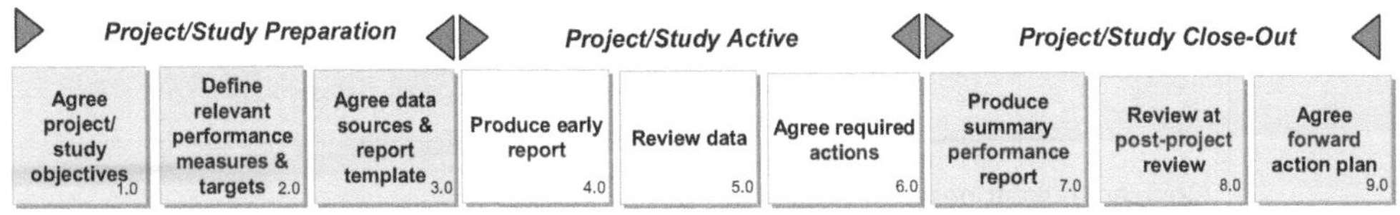

Figure 9.3 Outline performance management process: active phase

responsible for defining when this report will be produced, and for coordinating the production of this report, in collaboration with his or her CRO contacts. All CROs providing services to a given project or study should provide data as required. While many of the measures may not have any data at this early stage, it will test the process for generating data. This is particularly important where multiple vendors are being used in a single study or project. Furthermore, review of those data that are available will help the team 'test' the review process.

Sponsors are strongly advised to carefully consider the frequency of reports during the study and in particular requests for *ad-hoc* reports. Production of the latter can distract CRO staff from project delivery and can result in expensive change orders later on. The ideal is to have a project tracking tool that is accessible in real time to both sponsor and CRO staff, thereby negating the need for *ad-hoc* progress reports.

Step 5: Review data

How data contained in a performance report are reviewed can be a major driver of a successful outcome of a sponsor–CRO relationship. A well-designed performance management tool will allow the team to quickly identify missed targets or those 'at risk'. 'Traffic lights' are frequently used for this purpose:

- green indicates that all is on track
- amber indicates that targets are at risk
- red indicates that targets will definitely be, or have been, missed.

Targets, and therefore 'traffic light' thresholds, will be defined during the preparation phase. However, targets for many common metrics/KPIs can be standardised by individual companies. Where a balanced scorecard is used, most commercial packages can automatically generate 'traffic light reports' based on client-defined reporting thresholds. All amber and red traffic lights should be investigated to establish the underlying reason(s) why targets are at risk, or have been missed. Short narratives should be provided as explanation, and outlining remedial action being taken. A sample extract of a summary report is shown in Figure 9.4.

The narratives, as shown in Table 9.6, provide additional context around individual scores and are key to a balanced report. They should:

- be factual in nature and constructive in tone;
- clearly but briefly identify the issue and root cause, if known, or if unknown, state how the root cause will be identified; and
- briefly outline the action plan and who is accountable for its execution.

KPI	*Traffic light*	*Commentary required?*
Contract milestones		No
Key cycle		No
Quality		Yes

Figure 9.4 Example summary report

Table 9.6 Narrative explaining 'amber' traffic light on summary report

KPI/metric	*Brief description of issue and underlying cause*	*Action being taken or scheduled to be taken*	*Responsibility for resolution*
Quality	Data error rate >0.5%	Site training	M. Smith/J. Jones
	New site staff	Refresher schedule for w/c XXXXX	

Narratives should *not* be used to apportion blame.

Lead contacts from the sponsor and all CROs involved in the project should be given time to review the performance report prior to a discussion and the distribution list should have been agreed during study set-up. Naturally, most CROs will be reluctant for data on their performance to be shared with other CRO vendors working on the project and, for this reason, the report should be outcomes-based and not prejudicial to any CROs involved in the study.

Although teleconferencing may be appropriate later in the project, a face-to-face meeting is preferred for the first review, during which many issues may surface and the way in which the review is conducted will be critical in defining the tone of sponsor–CRO relationships going forward. Remember that the over-riding objective of performance management is to 'positively influence' execution of the project or study. Tables 9.7 and 9.8 show the ways in which report should and should not be reviewed.

Step 6: Agree required actions

The final step in reviewing the report is to agree and implement any interventions required to correct performance issues. These will simply be documented in the meeting minutes. Individuals will be allocated accountability for carrying out appropriate actions within an agreed timeframe.

Table 9.7 Preferred ways in which to review reports

What to do when reviewing the performance report
• Use the report on a *regular* basis to: – understand variations to expected performance and what is driving them – resolve any issues to alleviate future risks and improve performance and capabilities – learn from past performance – celebrate success.
• Review KPIs periodically to ensure that they drive the appropriate behaviours in line with strategic outsourcing goals.
• Ensure that the report drives an ACTION orientation at all times.

Table 9.8 Ways not to review reports

What NOT to do when reviewing the performance report
• Look for who to blame when there is a 'red/amber light': – Instead, leverage the joint sponsor–CRO team to find creative ways of resolving issues before they have an impact on performance. – If people associate 'red/amber light' with punishment, in time, no red/amber lights will be reported and the scorecard will cease to act as an early warning system.
• Hold people accountable for targets that they cannot influence.
• Focus solely on past performance – pay at least as much attention to indicators that reflect future performance.

The process outlined above will be carried out at various stages during the outsourcing project. As a minimum, the project team should evaluate performance on a quarterly basis, although some discussion of metrics will inevitably be included in more regular discussions.

During project/study close-out

A final performance review should always be conducted when the project or study has been completed, and the forum for doing this is usually termed the 'post-project review'. The benefits of conducting this review far outweigh the risk of it being perceived as a 'distraction' in the midst of other ongoing activities, for example, regulatory submissions, report writing, and so on. Providing that performance has been managed throughout the project/study, there should be no major 'surprises', in terms of performance levels achieved.

The post-project review allows sponsor and CRO team members to fully understand the levels of performance achieved, reasons for non-achievement of targets and to gain some insight into how to mitigate the risk of recurrence in the future. It is not enough for

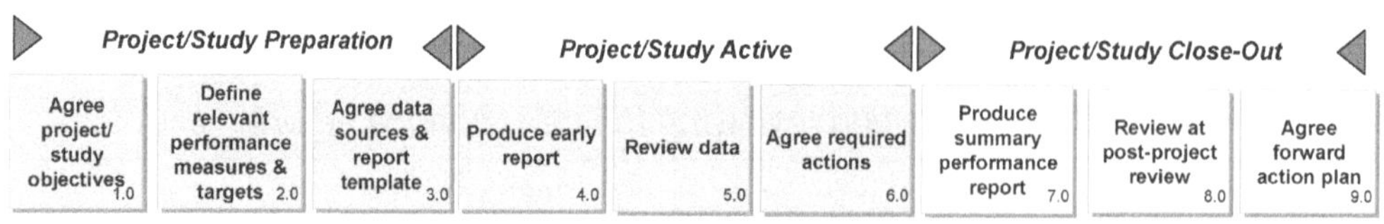

Figure 9.5 Outline performance management process: close-out phase

either party to walk away with a perception of a poor experience, and feeling reluctant to work together again. Most performance issues can be addressed constructively with the benefits being felt in future projects. Despite this, we often see a tendency to avoid a certain CRO after an unsuccessful project, resulting in the same painful learning curve with another vendor shortly afterwards.

The objectives of the post-project review are set out very clearly in guidelines issued by the Pharmaceutical Contract Management Group[3] and reproduced in Table 9.9.

Table 9.9 PCMG guidelines for post-project review

- To review and evaluate, in a timely fashion, all aspects of a trial run by the CRO, including metrics
- Establish the major strengths and weaknesses of the collaboration with a view to benefiting both the sponsor and the CRO, for future ventures, either jointly or with others
- To draw attention to any obvious deficiencies which would need to be rectified before the next contract work, both for the sponsor company and the CRO
- To pull together all the observations made by various diverse groups during the course of the programme
- To highlight training deficiencies within both the sponsor company and CRO, and to rectify these deficiencies
- To act as an *aide memoire* when consideration is being given to suitable CROs to perform another programme of work

Thorough preparation is critical for this meeting, and invitees should include:

- lead representatives from sponsor and all CROs involved in the project
- key project team members from sponsor and all CROs
- facilitator.

A facilitator who is external to the project team can help to direct the meeting, and capture any learning in a neutral way without a history of having worked within the team. The facilitator can also challenge the team to come up with solutions for working together in the future.

3. Source: PCMG Guidelines, August 2004.

Step 7: Produce summary performance report

A key input to the post-project review is the summary performance report. This looks similar to other reports produced during the project/study, but will contain cumulative and final data for all KPIs and metrics. It will show 'traffic lights' for all measures, and will contain narratives for all 'red' scores.

The report should be provided to all relevant individuals at least five working days prior to the post-project review.

Step 8: Review at post-project review

The post-project review meeting should always be face to face. A clear agenda will be set and distributed to all attendees at least five working days before the meeting. There will inevitably be several topics for discussion, including a review of the performance report. This review should be allocated sufficient time (at least one to two hours) and the following guidelines observed:

- Acknowledge and reward successes.
- Identify joint process improvements achieved and their value to both sponsor and CRO (mainly applies to strategic relationships).
- Identify deficiencies and explore root causes using the narratives provided and input from key team members.
- Do not allocate blame to individuals – focus on where processes and/or systems did not work and how these can be addressed in the future.

Processes and systems can fail at both sponsor and CRO, despite the best efforts of individuals involved. Open discussion of these failures and actions planned for the future can greatly improve relationships between the parties, particularly within the context of a strategic relationship. Within this type of relationship, a retrospective review of the project allows both CRO and sponsor to take remedial action and to reap the benefits in ongoing and future work.

Step 9: Agree forward action plan

Having reviewed the report and root causes of performance issues, the team will document any actions planned for the future. This can include recommendations to be implemented immediately on other ongoing projects. Specific actions should be assigned to individuals and it is important to also assign a target completion date to avoid the risk of post-study inertia!

A short summary of the actions agreed should be prepared and distributed to the following:

- sponsor–CRO relationship management team (where strategic relationships exist)
- CRO management (all relevant CROs)
- outsourcing management group (sponsor).

THE BALANCED SCORECARD AS A PERFORMANCE MANAGEMENT TOOL

One of the difficulties in managing performance is the selection of a performance management tool that is appropriate for the business context. There is a wide range of performance assessment tools available, varying from simple Excel-based worksheets to highly complex systems based on performance algorithms, and so on. In the context of outsourcing, it is important to choose a performance tool that:

- allows a company to assess the effectiveness of its outsourcing strategy;
- provides a way to measure all the business drivers associated with the need/decision to outsource; and
- enables clear identification and resolution of problem areas.

The balanced scorecard is one tool that meets these criteria.

The balanced scorecard has been with us since 1990 when Robert Kaplan and David Norton led a study of companies looking for new ways of measuring and managing performance. One of the main drivers for the study was the belief that purely financial measures of performance, the main measures used at that time, were inappropriate for modern organisations, particularly those that derive value from external (customer/supplier) interactions. The outcome of this work was the balanced scorecard. At the corporate level, it is essentially a framework that allows a company to translate its company-wide strategy into a coherent set of measures covering all areas of the business. It is 'balanced' in that it combines financial and non-financial, retrospective and prospective, and internal and external performance measures. If we refer back to the earlier quote from Lord Kelvin, the balanced scorecard tool allows us to define and measure performance in a range of areas, making the process of analysing performance much simpler.

The balanced scorecard has been described as a measurement system, a strategic management system and a communication tool. It is, quite simply, all three and is used by more than half of the Fortune 500 companies to manage performance at both a corporate level and across individual business units.

While the initial objective of the balanced scorecard was to assess and manage performance at the corporate level, it has also been used by business units and functional units to great effect. The common theme and driver of a successful outcome is that the company, business unit or functional strategy is clear.

Applying the balanced scorecard to clinical outsourcing

In 2002, Pharmacia Inc. redefined its global outsourcing strategy in Clinical Development. It set clear strategic targets relevant to the use of external CROs and selected a range of 'preferred providers'/CRO partners. Pharmacia chose an outsourcing balanced scorecard to manage implementation of the outsourcing strategy over a range of service areas. The company collaborated with all its CRO partners to agree the performance measures to be included, and performance targets that would be set. Most measures could be captured automatically from existing systems, for example, the CTMS or CDMS, and all were assigned a named 'owner' who served as the single point of contact for providing the relevant data.

Once implemented, the outsourcing balanced scorecard provided a means of assessing overall CRO performance and implementation of the outsourcing strategy, as well as allowing a comparative view of individual CRO providers. Mary Driver, then Global Head of Outsourcing at Pharmacia,[4] described the benefits of the outsourcing balanced scorecard as follows. It:

- allows performance management from a number of aspects;
- avoids the risk of 'management by anecdote';
- provides a consistent format for assessing performance;
- provides a forum for constructive feedback; and
- facilitates goal setting for future performance.

While Pharmacia Inc. implemented the balanced scorecard mainly within the context of strategic relationships with CROs, the tool is equally applicable to non-strategic relationships.

One important aspect of the balanced scorecard is that it is dynamic and should evolve over time. The measures included in a balanced scorecard will rarely be set in stone; remember that the tool is a means of measuring implementation of a defined strategy. Few strategies, including outsourcing strategies, remain static for long! Any shift in strategic direction should be accompanied by a review of the balanced scorecard, to ensure that appropriate performance measures continue to be used.

Finally, the balanced scorecard can be automated. There are several commercially available balanced scorecard tools, most of which can be customised to fit the outsourcing scenario. The choice of tool will often depend on the sponsor's existing technology architecture.

IMPLEMENTING A PERFORMANCE MANAGEMENT SYSTEM FOR CLINICAL OUTSOURCING

Implementing a new performance management system is always a challenge. Implementation of a system or tool that needs to work across organisational boundaries causes additional issues that need to be fully understood and factored into the plan.

Successful implementation of a performance management system will depend on the same factors as any other change project. These include:

4. May 18, 2002. Presentation at IIR Conference *Partnerships in Clinical Trials*, Amsterdam: 'Measuring the Results of Partnership through the Balanced Score Card Approach' and 'Keeping Score in Clinical Outsourcing', Driver, M.R. and Cuddigan, M., *SCRIP Magazine*, October 2002.

- *Definition and communication of a clear business case* – what are the objectives of the performance management system, and how does it link with the defined outsourcing strategy, if any? What types of outsourced work does it assess? Will it also link with internal performance management systems? What are the anticipated benefits? The answers to all of these questions should be clearly stated and communicated to all internal stakeholders of the system. A named senior manager should be available to address any questions from staff as they implement the new system.

- *Clear sponsorship and sustained leadership* – this is required of any business change. Senior-level leadership of the new system is critical for success. The simplest way of sponsors reinforcing this change is for them to require the output performance report to support all discussions of outsourced work. This way, staff members see the system being used within the ongoing management context. Furthermore, use of the performance tool should be a 'given' when negotiating new CRO contracts and the relevant performance measures specified in those contracts. Where the performance management tool/system is applied to CRO partnerships, sponsorship by management within the CRO is also critical to success. This factor is even more important in companies where previous change projects have not succeeded, thereby undermining credibility of future change efforts amongst staff.

- *Buy-in from all affected staff* – staff need to understand the value of the tool/system being implemented, for them and for their organisation. Failure to work on this aspect could lead to the system being viewed as causing more work for staff for the benefit of management only.

- *Availability of the required tools, support and training for all staff involved.* This should not be under-estimated. At the time the performance management process is launched to staff, it should be accompanied by a range of supporting material, including, for example:
  - one-page process overview – pocket-sized if possible
  - concise but comprehensive reference document outlining each step of the process, roles and responsibilities and any standard templates to be used. Where possible, this should be available on the corporate intranet to ensure access to the most current version at all times
  - *aide-memoire* to help discussions with CROs
  - names of individuals ('super-users') who can provide local, face-to-face support if needed.

- *A clear change control mechanism.* You should expect a new performance management approach/system to be updated as a result of experience in the first three to six months after implementation. This is not an indication of a sub-optimal system; rather an opportunity to incorporate learning from real-life implementation. The most common areas for change are:
  - reporting process steps – often streamlined after initial implementation
  - performance measures and reporting thresholds – should be reviewed and updated at least annually, but may need to be reviewed after the first three months of implementation, to ensure consistency with strategic objectives.

The change control mechanism should be clearly outlined in the reference document issued at launch, and maintained on the corporate intranet. Proposals for change may come from internal staff and from key CRO staff who can offer experience from a wide range of companies and situations. All proposed changes should be submitted to a nominated individual who will review proposals with senior managers in clinical development and outsourcing on a regular (probably quarterly) basis. Where a strategic relationship management structure exists with one or more CROs, any proposed changes should be discussed and agreed at one of the regular joint committee meetings.

SUMMARY

This chapter has set out some of the key challenges and assumptions related to managing performance when working with CROs. The first and most important factor to be considered is the strategy and rationale for outsourcing – in other words, what the use of CROs offers over and above existing internal capabilities. This may be short-term access to additional capacity, a long-term strategic outsourcing relationship based on access to specific capabilities, or some combination of both. Whichever is the case, the performance measures selected and managed should be directly related to the defined strategic objectives of the relationship. The processes outlined should be considered as proposals only; they should be tailored by each organisation as there is no single 'sure fire' approach that will work in all cases. Measurement of those aspects of the sponsor–CRO relationship that are relevant to a successful outcome provides a solid knowledge base on which performance can be assessed and improved jointly, on an ongoing basis. This will help ensure continued professional interactions between sponsor and CRO, and improve the overall climate related to outsourcing clinical development work.

Summary

Carl Emerson, *GSK Biologicals*, and Jean S. Edwards,
Eli Lilly UK
Pharmaceutical Contract Management Group (PCMG)

It is difficult to summarise all that we have read in the preceding chapters; there is no extra padding that could be whittled away from the concentrated messages carefully presented by this panel of experts. We have covered perceptive observations of practices inside the pharmaceutical industry, and insights from other industries too, descriptions of long-term strategic direction and tools for immediate practical help.

This book set out to guide future clinical outsourcing management philosophy and to be of instructional use to anyone encountering the outsourcing process for the first time, working with their first project. In addition, conscious of today's regulatory environment, the book aims to provide readers with the guidance and tools needed to ensure the outsourcing process will withstand regulatory scrutiny. In meeting these objectives, the authors have demonstrated that far from being an annex to the clinical trial process, the outsourcing function is undoubtedly a highly developed, advanced science. Thus, the book has something to offer all those who work in clinical drug development.

John Easton provided our first taste of the chapters to come with a thought-provoking introduction. John outlined how outsourcing had been employed in the early days to aid efficiency in the running of clinical trials, with effective cost drivers supporting the conversion of fixed costs to variable ones. In contrast, today's process is mature, developed to the stage where we optimise benefit through the careful use of balance sheet metrics. However, much has still to be done in the future to enable optimal drug development, and outsourcing should now be embedded in a model that meets strategic business needs. Certainly, outsourcing was used previously to manage capacity and control headcount, but today, even if only in small part, we are trialling the concept of extended outsourcing.

We were asked to consider whether the industry really understands the economic dimension of clinical outsourcing and to explain why, if we go to such lengths to select what we believe to be the 'best in breed', we still often treat CROs as if they were unskilled paid hands. In striving to optimise the outsourcing relationship, we were shown that we first need to investigate our core competencies objectively. Indeed, rather than be influenced by our organisation's internal view of what they think our core competencies are, we should discuss and agree what they need to be to meet the challenges of the current and future market place.

The industry has to find ways to reduce costs within the constraints of the regulatory environment, and so a focus on procuring quality is key. Outsourcing gives us access to an agile operating model in the service sector, but only if we can learn how to work effectively with these companies, and thus, we were introduced to a recurrent theme throughout this book: Relationship Management.

For many years, people have talked about the difference between tactical and strategic outsourcing without being particularly clear on two points; first, what this means, but secondly, and perhaps more tellingly, without being honest about the model in operation within the home office. Tactical has unfairly been perceived as a dirty word and, for many, strategic encompasses a broad church of sometimes poorly constructed solutions.

Thus it was important that our first chapter, from Smita Desai and Jeff Thomis, addressed the crucial question – 'If companies in other industries have strategies, why does the pharmaceutical market place linger so far behind?' It seems, we heard, that although drug developers operate in an immature market place, we have the opportunity to use outsourcing to effect profound change in our business practices. It means a change in attitudes, a change in behaviours – in short, a change in the whole relationship model. Is there something that we can learn from the virtual model? As companies get bigger through mega mergers, do we lose flexibility, adaptability and perhaps credibility?

Having painted a picture of the environment, we moved into more practical aspects of the process and Rikke Winther looked at CRO selection as required for both tactical and strategic outsourcing depending on the chosen model. Choosing a CRO needs a model for gaining an insight into the prospective organisation, and this chapter showed us how to look for the right skills, judge the relevant experience, and so select based on quality information from a variety of sources. We saw that the employment of more effort gave more reward, particularly if we were in it for a longer-term relationship. A series of questions, lined up against a detailed specification, is clearly a good starting place for successful CRO selection. However, we were once again warned of the need to focus on long-term solutions, that is to consider outcomes rather than immediate process.

The RFP process is foundational to successful contract placement and Emma Sabin carefully drew our attention to the key requirements in a logical, clear way. If we focus on our key drivers and what we are looking for at the end, then ensuring consistency enables coherent decision-making, based on clarity and a comprehensive specification.

Furthermore, we were shown that quality of our RFP leads to quality in the proposal and so through to the contract, an important lesson for those trying to squeeze the critical early stages of a newly proposed protocol for outsourcing. The key components of the package were described and the chapter ably demonstrated the need to establish what the key cost drivers are, and to understand that cost does not represent the whole picture. We need to recognise that there is a time, cost and quality triangle and that while pressure on one or two is possible, pressure on all three is not. As the increasing influence of professional procurement experts continues to drive increasing professionalism in the outsourcing executive, this is an important message to remember. As a feature of this, we were reminded of how important proper, careful feasibility was, and time needs to be built into the process if this is going to be anything more than a paper exercise. We saw more of this in the chapter on contract models.

Once again we were reminded of the important regulatory environment within which we all operate; at all times responsibility for compliance with regulations lies with the sponsor organisation, and furthermore, we need to specify which roles and responsibilities are being transferred. In conclusion, we were urged to think why we were outsourcing and to focus accordingly.

Risk management in clinical development is beginning to be taken more seriously. It is an important consideration for almost any endeavour and Nermeen Varawalla showed us how important it is when working with CROs and other suppliers. In this chapter we learnt how both parties have risks, but that these are different and need to be mutually understood. For effective management, risks need to be clearly identified, managed through a variety of potential mechanisms and mitigated. Making the right decision and supporting it through having the right contract helps, but once again, the importance of relationship management was highlighted as key to ensuring we obtain the full potential value from our outsourcing.

Jim Cannon is an experienced professional, training, negotiating and working around the globe. In recent years, he has worked with the PCMG to put together a training programme specially tailored to meet the needs of the outsourcing manager and, in Chapter 5, Jim gives simple examples of a multiplicity of techniques and practical tools covering a variety of different approaches to negotiation. Each has its place, and knowing the full range of options available to you and your counterpart will enable better decision-making and more effective management when confronted by different situations and individuals.

We next turned with Alan Morgan to the different contract types and saw how all the previous investment gets cemented together; important here was the linking of fees and payment to the company's corporate philosophy and strategy. While this might appear obvious, we need to beware the trap of processing things in the same way as always, and of maintaining the *status quo* without thinking where we are going. We should always be aware of the need to challenge the current approach to ensure that it supports our final direction. Different services and different sorts of work are best supported by different contracts, and we looked at examples of these. It is important that we think of our end object and implement the language that will achieve this. Sub-contractors, change orders and a relationship that supports a master services agreement as opposed to something for a single service, were all discussed, as was an introduction to important concepts such as earned value analysis.

Legal language puts the agreement and style into words that give commitment and clarity to all that has gone before. While contracts can appear a foreign language to many of us, Paul Ranson showed us, in simple words, the difference of emphasis between countries, matters of history and harmonisation and finished with an explanation of the clauses, what they mean and what it is important to consider when compiling an agreement.

Unfortunately, regardless of how good the contract, both in terms of legal language and project specification, we heard from Nadia Turner that the leading cause of partnership failure was that of a damaged relationship. Strategic relationship management (SRM) is a structure mechanism designed to optimise the value of a relationship. SRM has several components and the detail of their implementation will depend on the importance of the partnership and the size of the organisation(s) involved. We were introduced to the concept of key account manager and the role of the relationship manager, but were warned that despite this being a concept still in its infancy, we could expect more changes in the environment if we are able to rise to the challenges facing the industry.

Our final chapter, by Michelle Cuddigan and Sarah King, demonstrated the importance of measuring the success of the process mastered in the preceding chapters through appropriate performance management techniques. A detailed analysis of the current state of the art, with emphasis on the importance to both parties of the collection of routine metrics and limited key performance indicators, followed. We were encouraged to have a plan, to measure throughout the project life and to follow the example of more than half of the Fortune 500 companies by implementing the effective use of a balanced scorecard. Once again we saw that our object needed to be our project outcome, and that selective use of measures should be tailored towards the strategic objectives of the relationship.

If we are to realise the vision stated in the introduction of cutting costs by 30 to 40 per cent, it will not be by petty wrangling over individual line items in a proposed budget, but through the use of a well-thought-out, detailed resourcing strategy that analyses the long-term view of the key cost drivers, understands the risks and core competencies necessary for the best pharmaceutical teams to develop life-saving drugs, and the contractual model with suppliers to support this. Above it all will sit a structured, planned relationship, measured and managed by experienced people in companies with the vision to see beyond this year's costs budget to the needs of the decade to come.

The outsourcing professional of the future is not a scientist on the periphery of the clinical trials process, but a trained, disciplined, competent strategist, grounded on years of experience, equipped with practical tools for implementation of best practice, with an eye, not on the pounds to be saved today, but focused on best value achieved by continued progress from first contact to final contract delivery under an umbrella of sustainable relationship management.

This book has shown us the way ahead, building on expertise currently available in the industry. It also shows us that the coming years promise to be exciting ones for all involved in outsourcing clinical development.

The PCMG

The PCMG (Pharmaceutical Contract Management Group) was founded in 1994 and is a professionally constituted body dedicated to optimising outsourcing performance in drug development for its members and their companies.

PCMG is aiming to build upon its achievements to become the leading forum in Europe for the discussion of outsourcing issues.

Today, there are more than 70 members based in 12 European countries from 45 companies. These members come from a wide spectrum of organisations, including traditional pharma, biotechnology and virtual development companies.

The PCMG are very aware that maximising the success of a pharmaceutical company's outsourcing strategy and reducing the risks of using a third party is of critical importance. It is with these challenges in mind that the activities and programme of events are developed, to support the membership with every aspect of the outsourcing process.

Each year they hold a number of workshops covering a wide spectrum of key topics affecting the business. Recent workshops have covered:

- third party providers
- CRO evaluation and management
- contracts
- the outsourcing function – best practice and future trends affecting our role
- outsourcing strategies
- cost
- relationship management.

These workshops not only provide an opportunity to listen but also to network in an informal setting with colleagues from other companies.

The PCMG have also produced outsourcing role competencies. These have proved very useful to members in developing company-specific competencies for their roles, which can sometimes be unique. The PCMG also supports the development of competencies with a series of training courses designed to support learning and development in key skill areas associated with outsourcing.

For further information regarding our future workshops and training please call Samantha Dignan on +44 (0)1625 267 879 or visit www.pcmg.org.uk.

Index

For Product Safety Concerns and Information please contact our EU representative GPSR@taylorandfrancis.com Taylor & Francis Verlag GmbH, Kaufingerstraße 24, 80331 München, Germany